Is Conservatism Dead?

John Gray is a Fellow of Jesus College and Professor of Politics at Oxford University and has been visiting professor at Harvard and Yale Universities. He is one of the most distinguished social theorists writing today. He has a regular column in the *Guardian* and writes and reviews frequently for other papers and journals.

He is the author of several books including *Post-liberalism* (1991), *Beyond the New Right* (1994), *Berlin* (1995), *Enlightenment's Wake* (1995) and *Endgames* (1997). He is currently working on a book on the utopia of the global free market, *False Dawn* which will be published by Granta in March 1998.

David Willetts is MP for Havant and Conservative Employment Spokesman. He is now working with Peter Lilley on the review of Conservative policy following the 1997 general election defeat.

He served as an official in HM Treasury from 1978 to 1984, including a spell as Private Secretary to Nigel Lawson. He was a member of Mrs Thatcher's Downing Street Policy Unit from 1984 to 1986. From 1987 to 1992 he was Director of Studies at the Centre for Policy Studies. In 1992 he was elected as MP for Havant, Hampshire. During the last parliament he served as a Government Whip and as Paymaster General in the Cabinet Office.

He has been closely involved in the development of Conservative Party policy over the ⎯⎯⎯⎯⎯⎯⎯⎯⎯⎯⎯⎯⎯⎯⎯⎯⎯⎯⎯ economic and social ⎯⎯⎯⎯⎯⎯⎯⎯⎯⎯⎯⎯⎯⎯⎯⎯ *onservatism* (1992).

Is Conservatism Dead?

JOHN GRAY & DAVID WILLETTS

PROFILE BOOKS

First published in Great Britain by Profile Books in association
with the Social Market Foundation.

Profile Books Ltd
62 Queen Anne Street
London WIM 9LA

The Social Market Foundation
11 Tufton Street
London SWIP 3QB

Printed in Great Britain by Biddles Ltd

A CIP catalogue record for this book is available from the British Library

ISBN 1 86197 042 0

Contents

Foreword

When the Social Market Foundation first published John Gray's *The Undoing of Conservatism* and *Civic Conservatism* by David Willetts it did so with the intention of sparking a debate about the future of conservatism or indeed about whether conservatism had a future at all. Both questions are especially pertinent now, in light of the recent general election, and both authors have updated their contributions. They are published here as a single volume for the first time.

In *The Undoing of Conservatism* John Gray, one of the most influential moral philosophers of his generation and a neo-liberal apostate, contended that the increasing domination of conservative thought by market liberalism had boxed it into a corner. Conservatism was unable to advance policies which threatened further social instability and incapable of retreating to a moral fundamentalism which progress had rendered obsolete. In his view recent events have only added weight to his original argument. The Conservatives, he says, after allowing themselves to be captured by New Right ideology have now gone the way of all ideological parties. Lacking an adequate response to the social and economic changes which they helped to bring about they have found themselves outflanked by a non-ideological Labour Party governing from the radical centre. In retrospect, says Gray, the domestic victory of Thatcherism over socialism and the end of the Cold War abroad were decisive moments for the

New Right only in the sense that they were a portent of its own downfall. Seen like this, the result on May 1st 1997 was 'an inescapable nemesis. It was the fate of a party undone by ideological hubris.'

It remains unclear from Gray's analysis whether conservatism could have done anything to avoid this fate. Had it remained exclusively a One Nation movement in the mould of Butler, Macmillan and Macleod it might still have been swept away by the tide of events. As Gray himself says, the Tories cannot go back to being a party of tradition in a post-traditional society or else they risk becoming the representatives of a new 'rainbow coalition' of disaffected right wing minority groups. Perhaps his most serious charge is that by embracing the virtues of the free market as vigorously as they did, conservatives appeared to be saying that social cohesion was some fortunate by-product of the prosperity generated by a market economy. This progressively disconnected them from the silent majority which cared as much about controlling economic risk and the future of public services as it did about rising incomes and lower personal taxation.

It is this caricature of contemporary conservatism which David Willetts set out to dispel in *Civic Conservatism*. As the leading writer on the subject of his time, Willetts said that it was the growth of government not the gales of globalisation which had done most to undermine civil society and its institutions. Looking back, Willetts admits that the Labour Party was able to portray free market conservatism as the destructive force which Gray talks about. More than that, Labour touched a nerve when it said that economic performance relied on social cohesion and 'community'. People want more choice, better services and a higher standard of living; but they also want continuity and cohesion. The two do not always go together. For Willetts, the essence of conservatism is how one manages the resulting tensions.

What is the appropriate framework within which a commitment to free markets and a sense of social obligation can be reconciled? For Margaret Thatcher it was her religious beliefs. But Willetts concedes that in an increasingly secular world, conservatism has to look beyond religion for some other point of reference. Labour has stumbled on 'community', a bland abstraction which stresses equity and fairness but which is difficult to locate in the real world. The concept of 'community' and of communitarianism ignores the fact that universal principles do not always apply in the particular – one American academic described it as wanting Salem without the witches. Willetts prefers flesh and blood institutions. For all of their complications and loyalties, he says that 'institutions find it easier to tolerate each other than communities do'. The coming years will be marked by how much autonomy these institutions are allowed to have.

In essence, Gray and Willetts map out the philosophical battleground of the post-Thatcher era. Who or what is best equipped to deal with the uncertainties wrought by social and economic change? For Gray, the Conservative Party has disqualified itself because it is a victim of the very change which it helped to bring about. Creating and maintaining social cohesion is the stuff of non-ideological politics and the only proponent of that for the foreseeable future is

Labour. Willetts sees things differently. Managing change cannot be done centrally nor should it be attempted solely through politics. For him, politics is a subset of democracy which must include a thriving civil society with multifarious institutions that lie wholly or partly outside the realm of the political process. So can the problems this country faces be resolved by more politics or eased by less of it? The answer depends on whom you find the more convincing.

Roderick Nye
October 1997

Part 1:
The Undoing of
Conservatism

1: Conservatism in Retrospect

The undoing of conservatism has come about as an unintended consequence of Hayekian policy. The hegemony, within conservative thought and practice, of neo-liberal ideology has had the effect of destroying conservatism as a viable political project in our time. Traditional conservatism is no longer a realistic political option when inherited institutions and practices have been swept away by the market forces which neo-liberal policies release or reinforce. When our institutional inheritance – that precious and irreplaceable patrimony of mediating structures and autonomous professions – is thrown away in the pursuit of a managerialist cultural revolution seeking to remodel the entire national life on the impoverished model of contract and market exchange, it is clear that the task of conserving and renewing a culture is no longer understood by contemporary conservatives. In the context of such a Maoism of the Right, it is the permanent revolution of unfettered market processes, not the conservation of traditional institutions and professions, each having a distinctive ethos, that has become the ruling project of contemporary conservatism. At the same time, neo-liberalism itself can now be seen as a self-undermining political project. Its political success depended upon cultural traditions and constellations of interests that neo-liberal policy was bound to dissipate. In adopting the neo-liberal programme of a permanent institutional revolution as their own, contemporary conservatives have not only abandoned any claim to be guardians of continuity in national life; they have at the same time linked their fortunes to a political project which all the evidence suggests is self-defeating.

In the late 1970s, and throughout the earlier years of the 1980s, neo-liberalism was a compelling response to otherwise intractable dilemmas. The manifest failings of corporatist policy in Britain and the collapse of central planning throughout the Soviet bloc vindicated market institutions as the chief organising structures in any modern economy. The old 'systems debate', between 'planning' and 'markets', was resolved decisively on the terrain of history. By the late 1980s, however, that old debate receded, and a new one began to emerge – a debate about the varieties and limits of market institutions and their cultural and political preconditions. In this new debate, neo-liberal thought has little to contribute. Further, conservative policy that is animated by neo-liberal ideology finds itself baffled and powerless when confronted by the political challenges to market institutions that distinguish the 1990s – well exemplified in the success of neo-communist parties as the principal political beneficiaries of market reform in the post-Soviet world. In Western democracies, such as Britain, Canada and New Zealand, conservative parties animated by free market ideology look, impotent and aghast, into an electoral abyss which their own policies have opened up for them. Yet the option of returning to an older conservatism – 'One Nation' Toryism in Britain, say – has been closed for them by the social effects of market forces whose often destructive radicalism conservative policies have only enhanced. As a result conservatism, in Britain and elsewhere, has arrived at an intellectual and political impasse from

4

which it can neither advance nor retreat. Except in societies such as Italy, whose special histories have given it a further lease on life, conservatism is now a spent force in most Western countries. In an irony that will delight historians in years to come, the political effect of the ephemeral intellectual hegemony of the New Right, in Britain and similar countries, has probably been to accomplish the political destruction of conservatism: it may have rendered conservative parties unelectable, perhaps for a generation.

The capture of conservative parties and governments throughout the Western world by free market ideology was an accomplished and familiar fact by the late 1980s. Its full implications have yet to be properly understood. The conquest of modern Western conservatism by a species of market fundamentalism — Manchesterism *redivivus* — has transformed it profoundly and probably irreversibly. A political outlook, that in Burke, Disraeli and Salisbury was sceptical of the project of the Enlightenment and suspicious of the promise of progress, has mortgaged its future on a wager on indefinite economic growth and unfettered market forces. Such a bet — Hayek's wager, as it might be called — hardly exhibits the political prudence once revered as a conservative virtue. It leaves the governments and societies that have staked their patrimony on such a throw defenceless and without resources when, in the normal fortunes of markets everywhere, or because economic growth has come up against insuperable social or ecological limits, market institutions fail to deliver the goods expected of them. In such circumstances, liberal civilization itself may be imperiled, insofar as its legitimacy has been linked with the utopia of perpetual growth powered by unregulated market processes, and the inevitable failure of this utopia spawns illiberal political movements.

Indeed, unconstrained market institutions are bound to undermine social and political stability, particularly as they impose on the population unprecedented levels of economic insecurity with all the resultant dislocations of life in families and in communities. Market-driven economic change, especially when it is large-scale, rapid and unremitting, also fosters insecurity by marginalising traditional forms and confounding established expectations. In Europe, the emergence of high levels of structural unemployment has been accompanied by the re-emergence of atavistic parties of the Right. In Britain, the desolation of communities by unchannelled market forces and the resultant pervasive sense of economic insecurity have not evoked similar illiberal political movements, nor are they likely to; but they have been crucial factors in an epidemic of crime that has probably no parallel in national life since the early nineteenth century. It is only by the exercise of heroic powers of self-deception, or else by simple dishonesty, that British Conservatives can fail to discern the links between levels of criminality unprecedented in recent generations and policies of marketisation, pursued for over a decade and a half, which have ridden roughshod over settled communities and established expectations. It is only a similar exercise in self-delusion or economy with the truth that can blind Conservatives to the links between the economic changes which their policies reinforced and accelerated and the growth of the many forms of poverty, indifferently lumped together under the fashionable but deeply misconceived category of the underclass.

It is a general truth that, when disembedded from any context of common life and emancipated from political constraints, market forces – especially when global – work to unsettle communities and to delegitimate traditional institutions. This is a truism, no doubt; but it expresses an insight – that for most people, security against risk is more important than the enhancement of choice – that conservative parties and governments have forgotten. For many people, perhaps most, the largely illusory enhancement of choice through freeing-up markets does not compensate for the substantial increase in insecurity it also generates. More specifically, neo-liberal policies have extended to the middle classes the insecurities and risks that have always plagued working-class life. By framing their policies with reference to an Enlightenment ideology of world-betterment through unconstrained global markets, Western conservatives may have given the *rentier* a new lease on life; but they have also brought about the euthanasia of the old middle classes. The political price to be paid for this dubious achievement is likely to be high, and, in the British case, may conceivably be the destruction of the Conservative Party - in its present form at any rate – as a potential party of government.

In throwing in its lot with the cult of the free market, Western conservatism has colluded with the spirit of the age, well summarised in Hayek's candidly nihilistic dictum, 'Progress is movement for movement's sake'.[1] Conservatives who imagine their parties can re-appropriate traditional values are deluding themselves. New political groupings may arise, in which genuinely conservative ideas coexist with, and are fertilised by, ideas from other traditions; but the notion that established conservative parties can be reclaimed, and turned into vehicles for an older conservative philosophy is, in most countries, a mere illusion. The result of conservative policy over the past decade and a half has been to junk traditional practices of all sorts in the pursuit of the mirage of the wholly free market; the evident fact that the workings of unconstrained market institutions might be incompatible with the stability of any real-world society is treated as a taboo in conservative political discourse. Equally, the possibility – indeed, the reality – that policies predicated on the prospect of open-ended economic growth neglect the fragility of the natural world of which our species is but a part has been thoroughly exorcised from consciousness. In attaching themselves to the utopia of perpetual growth in goods and services, conservatives have surrendered abjectly to the spirit of the age. To attempt to return conservative parties, or for that matter Western societies, to traditional forms of life at this stage in our history is to tilt at windmills, or else enter into a dangerous flirtation with forms of cultural fundamentalism whose upshot will be – like the ephemeral 'Back to Basics' campaign of the Major government – at best farcical. The better way lies in the recognition that in our circumstances renewing genuine conservative values, and passing on the traditions of a liberal civilization, demand novel and radical policies and a willingness to think in unorthodox ways. Contemporary conservative thought is of no more assistance in this task than traditional socialist thought.

A central test of the readiness to think fresh thoughts is the way we think about market institutions. On the view defended here they are not ends in themselves but means or tools whose end is human well-being. Those who apply the model of the free market that was useful in the struggle against the stagnant corporatism of the 1970s to the radically different problems of the 1990s are misapplying liberal ideas in a fashion that is dangerous to liberal civilization itself. If the threat to a liberal form of life in the 1970s came from an invasive and overly ambitious state, in the 1990s it comes from the desolation and collapse of communities and the excesses of individualism, which have been compounded by policies which see marketisation as an all-purpose cure for economic and social ills. If, in the 1970s, the principal danger to liberal civilization came from the hubris of government, in the 1980s and 1990s it has come from hubristic liberal ideology, in which an obsession is made of individual choice and the needs of solidarity and common life go unrecognised or spurned. The starting point for serious political discourse in Britain in the 1990s must be in the recognition that the paleo-liberal celebration of consumer choice and market freedom as the only undisputed values has become a recipe for *anomie*, social breakdown and ultimately economic failure.

This is not to say there are not areas of policy in which market institutions can still be usefully extended: there is a good case, as I shall suggest in Chapter 7, for the introduction of a version of the educational voucher that is different in crucial respects from those proposed by neo-liberals, with the aim of anchoring schooling more deeply in local communities. And, provided such measures are fully and properly funded, there may be a useful role for analogous voucher schemes in some areas of welfare policy. Equally, not all curbs on market freedoms presently in place or currently envisaged are sensible, or defensible in any terms that are recognisably liberal. In recent EU proposals – for the restriction of vitamins as forms of prescription medicine and for the restraint of commercial expression, for example – there is much that smacks of the moralism and paternalism that would immediately, and rightly, be rejected by liberal opinion in other areas of policy.[2] From the truth that market freedom is not a dogma, it does not follow that current or proposed restraints on market freedoms are always acceptable. The deeper truth is that market institutions are useful devices, not articles of faith. Their scope, varieties and limits cannot be known a priori, but are to be assessed tentatively and provisionally. Such assessment will turn on the contribution they make to human well-being and their impact on valuable cultural traditions and forms of common life. Importantly, since cultural forms are various, the proper scope and limits of market freedoms will also be variable. Abstract notions of choice or rights are of very little use in sensible reflection on markets and their limits. Consumer choice, for example, is an important good, still sometimes wrongly curtailed, whose justification is in its contribution to individual empowerment. Nevertheless it cannot be the basis of an entire political philosophy, or of the whole agenda of public policy.

When applied, or misapplied, in the context of a neo-liberal ideology that is insensitive to the human needs for community and cultural identity, the idea of consumer choice becomes positively pernicious. To make a fetish of free trade, for example, when it manifestly does not serve human needs, risks discrediting market institutions and endangers the stability of liberal societies. Yet this risk will become a reality wherever market institutions are presented not as indispensable instruments for the achievement of individual and communal objectives, to be shaped and curbed by reference to those ends, but as an all-or-nothing package, which has only an incidental (or coincidental) connection with the communities and cultures it serves. The real danger of paleo-liberal thought and policy in all its forms is that it does not understand that market institutions are stable and enduring only insofar as they are embedded in the common cultures of those whose needs they exist to serve.

This is a danger that is being incurred not only by free market conservatism but also by traditional varieties of the Left project, all of which stake their policies on a resumption of economic growth – on a species of revived Croslandism. Insofar as the Left project remains wedded to 'growthmanship', and fails to respond to the challenge of a situation in which a resumption of economic growth on conventional lines is unachievable or undesirable, it will suffer the same fate of political obsolescence that has befallen the market liberal doctrines of the New Right. Nor have recent attempts to reformulate a New Left project confronted the obstacles to socialist ideals presented by conventional prescriptions for global free trade.[3] At present, all conventional political thought seems fixated on assumptions, such as the possibility and desirability of resuming economic growth at the rates and of the sorts experienced in the 1960s or the 1980s, and on models, such as those of Anglo-American individualist capitalism or European social democracy, which have clearly had their day. There is a real danger that the ossification of liberal thought resulting from the hegemony of discredited neo-liberal ideas in all mainstream parties opens a window of political opportunity for avowed enemies of liberal civilization. We will best conserve our liberal patrimony if, as Maynard Keynes urged us to do, we seek new wisdom for a new age. The beginning of such wisdom is in the recognition that Western conservatism has come undone in its adoption of the policies and philosophy of the unfettered free market.

2: The Strange Death of Free Market Conservatism

What must be true for conservatism to be possible? This question is likely to be seen as a donnish diversion from serious political thought. Its implication – that whatever the preconditions of conservatism may be, they may no longer exist among us today – may seem especially frivolous. Virtually all countries in the West have political parties that avow themselves to be conservative; there are, or have been lately, groups which meet to consider the principles of conservative philosophy; and it has been cogently argued by one of our most modern and least nostalgic writers that a conservative disposition remains an essential element in any life that is recognisable by us, where the passion for novelty and the penchant for choice-making are notably strong, as worth living.[4] Given these familiar considerations, an inquiry into the presuppositions of conservatism may well appear to be ill-considered. And certain well-known features of conservative thought would seem to make an exploration of its general preconditions an especially unpromising venture. After all, what could be more misconceived than an effort at a transcendental deduction of a political outlook that disdains abstract principle, favours the local over the universal, and denies that practice needs support from philosophical 'foundations'? The search for the necessary preconditions of conservatism may even be dismissed as arising from a misunderstanding of conservatism itself.

Yet it will be my contention that the question with which I began is far from frivolous. I will argue instead that the conditions under which conservatism as a coherent form of political thought and practice are possible no longer exist; that conservatism has for us a Cheshire cat quality, in that what it proposes to conserve is a spectral thing, voided of substance, partly by the policies of recent conservative governments and partly by aspects of modern societies which such policies have reinforced; and that conservative parties and movements have in all Western countries been captured by neo-liberal ideas, more properly thought of as those of fundamentalist or classical liberalism, which in their utopian projects of world-improvement and their expectation of convergence on a universal civilization are alien to the forms of thought and practice most characteristic of a conservative outlook as that used to be understood.

At the same time, I will propose any political outlook that is merely reactionary in its response to the dilemmas of the late modern period in which we live, is bound to be a form of quixotry, or else of atavism. Ironically, and ominously, it is the seduction of conservative parties by a primitive species of paleo-liberalism – which is what neo-liberalism and neo-conservatism really are – that enhances the prospects of truly atavistic illiberal movements. In a mirror irony, the hegemony of market liberalism within conservative thought and practice, when combined with the disruptive effects of unfettered market forces on settled communities and inherited social forms, means that unreflective adherence to tradition has been destroyed and replaced, if at all, by varieties of religious or cultural fundamentalism. In short, the subversive effects of unhampered market institutions on traditional forms of life makes free-market conservatism an inherently unstable and, over time, a self-undermining political project. For these reasons, I conclude that a genuinely conservative form of political thought and practice, the lineaments of which we can discern as at least one element in our cultural history, is no longer a real possibility for us. How has this strange circumstance come about?

3: The Self-destruction of Traditional Conservatism

The conquest in the 1980s of conservative parties throughout the world by doctrines of market liberalism did not come out of the blue. Since the end of the Second World War at least, conservative parties in Western countries relied upon policies which stimulated economic growth as the principal means of securing the political legitimacy of market institutions. In conditions of rapid economic growth the destructive impact of market forces on communities and settled practices is softened, or compensated by, the new opportunities that such growth affords. Further, the dislocations occasioned by market competition can in such conditions be alleviated by welfare institutions and more fundamental issues of distribution and livelihood taken off the political agenda. This was, in effect, the Butskellite settlement in post-war British political life: social conflict was avoided by the pursuit of a full employment policy and by the establishment of a welfare state in which the middle classes participated fully, both funded by the proceeds of economic growth. Post-war British governments until 1979 considered their task as that of extending their hold on office by aligning the electoral and the political cycles in a context of sustained economic growth. Whether or not particular governments were successful in this feat, the adoption of the conception by the two major parties in Britain produced a period of political and social stability that began to unravel only in the late 1970s. Moreover, the post-war settlement in Britain was paralleled by similar settlements in all major Western countries, which in many of them began to show signs of strain in the late 1970s and early 1980s.

The chief innovation of early Thatcherism in Britain was to tear up this post-war social agreement – at least insofar as it concerned macro-economic policies aimed at full employment and at a smooth meshing of the economic and political cycles – and adopt the Medium Term Financial Strategy (MTFS). The welfare state was left comparatively intact, but the political thrust of early Thatcherism was in the direction of the dismantlement of the corporatist policies of the 1960s and early 1970s, by the dissolution of the triangular relationship between government, business and the trade unions on which they were based. It is important to note that these corporatist relationships started to come unstuck in Britain well before the coming to power of Margaret Thatcher in 1979. The Healey-IMF squeeze of the last Labour government was a clear portent of the fiscal austerity pursued in the early Thatcher years. It is no less important to be clear that when the collusive corporatism of the 1960s and 1970s foundered it was because it had resulted in stagflation and social conflict, rather than yielding steady economic growth and social peace. Corporatism had failed to deliver the goods; but the idea that market institutions can only secure political legitimacy in a democratic regime against a background of steady growth in output, remained firmly in place. The central project of early Thatcherism, whose intellectual inspiration came from rational expectations theory in economics, the utopian notion of an economic constitution proposed in the Public Choice school and the *mélange* of classical liberal and libertarian ideas that came together briefly under the heading of the New Right, was to secure the conditions of economic growth by setting up a stable framework of rules rather than by government acting directly as a pacemaker of economic expansion.

Though, predictably, the MTFS came to grief in the mid-1980s, the rewriting of the British social compact it embodied had a political resonance into the early 1990s. It is arguable that the 1992 general election result can be better explained by the decoupling in voters' perceptions of the performance of government from that of the economy than by mistrust of Labour's economic competence. This decoupling, in turn, was probably the most enduring trace of over a decade of Thatcherite rhetoric and statecraft focusing on the autonomy of market forces – a tribute to the success of Thatcherism, for a while at least, as a hegemonic political project whose objective was the transformation of British political culture. This disassociation also held true in the 1997 general election when the strong economy failed to guarantee the Conservatives' re-election. Whether this alteration in voters' perceptions is in fact irreversible or even long-lasting is another matter, but fortunately not one which anything fundamental in the present argument turns on. For, even if the correlation between voting behaviour and perceived economic well-being has been irreversibly weakened in British political life, the electoral prospects of British conservatism are not thereby necessarily enhanced. An upswing in the economy does not inevitably work in favour of a sitting Conservative government, as elections turn on other issues. Most likely, the traces of this Thatcherite legacy, in conjunction with the stubborn reality of persistently slow growth, will alter the terms of political trade by shifting the content of public discourse in Britain. The parties will be assessed by the voters on how they address issues on the quality of life rather than narrow issues of economic management. Specifically, they will be judged on how they propose to protect the quality of life in Britain more than their policies for the rekindling of economic growth. In other words, low growth – an annual growth rate of around 2 per cent or so, say – seems likely to be a presupposition of political debate in Britain, as perhaps in other European countries, for the foreseeable future. This is a prospect that bodes ill for the political fortunes of conservatism insofar as it continues to be wedded to the growth-oriented doctrines of market liberalism.

The deepest difficulty of contemporary conservatism is that of securing the political legitimacy of the unfettered market institutions to which it is committed, in an age of low economic growth. In such an age, the gale of creative destruction blows less benignly, as the processes of entrepreneurship and technological innovation which distinguish unencumbered market institutions eliminate jobs without generating new ones of the same sort or at the same rate. The dystopian prospect – not so far away, perhaps, from the present reality – is of a highly dynamic but low-growth economy in which a permanent revolution in technologies and productive arrangements yields large-scale structural unemployment and pervasive job insecurity. As Edward Luttwak has noted, in his provocative piece on 'Why Fascism is the Wave of the Future':

> structural change, with all its personal upheavals and
> social disruptions, is now quite rapid even when there is
> zero growth, becoming that much faster when
> economies do grow. The engine turns, grinding lives
> and grinding down established human relationships, even
> when the car is stopped; and reaches Ferrari-like rpms at
> the most modest steamroller speeds ... neither the
> moderate Right nor the moderate Left even recognises,
> let alone offers any solution for, the central problem of
> our days: the completely unprecedented personal
> economic insecurity of working people, from industrial
> workers and white-collar clerks to medium-high
> managers.[5]

The fact that the subversive dynamism of market institutions, particularly when they are globalised, destroys personal and communal economic security even in conditions of zero economic growth is of central importance not only in the Western liberal democracies of which Luttwak is speaking primarily, but also for the post-communist states. For, in the latter, the collapse of bankrupt institutions of central planning, and the subsequent ill-conceived adoption of neo-liberal policies of shock therapy, has replicated in grotesquely exaggerated form the Western problem of market-driven structural economic adjustments occurring in conditions of zero or even negative growth. Entirely predictably, though it evokes the baffled incomprehension of Western opinion, the political beneficiaries of mass economic insecurity pervasive in such conditions have, virtually everywhere, been neo-communist and neo-fascist parties, sometimes in combination. In many, indeed most of the post-communist states, the political risk of unregulated market institutions that are exposed to the full gale of global market forces – namely that the liberal institutions that are supposed (according to Western theory) to accompany them will be repudiated or compromised – has already generated a powerful backlash against Western-imposed policies of shock therapy. It is paradoxical, but typical of the intellectual confusion of the times, that politicians and parties in the post-communist countries that seek to temper the impact of market reform on an already shell-shocked society, and thereby preserve a measure of social and political stability, are denounced by Western conservatives for their deviations from neo-liberal orthodoxy. These developments in the post-communist countries have so far been little noted or comprehended in the West. They contain lessons that Western political élites and opinion formers show few signs of learning. The fundamental truth that rapid and continuous market-driven economic change is inimical to settled community, and in the longer run to the stability of liberal and democratic institutions, has apparently yet to be grasped by most Western policy makers.

The fact that the mobility of labour required of everyone in a society dominated by unconstrained market institutions is profoundly disruptive of settled communities and imposes severe strains on life in families is neglected, or repressed, by those contemporary conservatives – the vast majority – for whom the United States is the tacit or explicit model. It is true enough that, in the American case, all other values have been sacrificed for the sake of micro-economic flexibility, productivity and low labour costs. This American model, which is unlikely to be replicated as successfully anywhere else, has to its credit that the relentless pursuit of efficiency has kindled renewed economic growth, has spurred technological advance and generated millions of new jobs. At the same time, the American model of individualist market institutions has been distinguished by levels of family breakdown and fractured community, criminality and incarceration that are unknown in other Western countries. In addition, the successes in job creation in America have necessitated a large-scale casualisation of work, a lowering of real incomes in the middle classes and a revolution of falling expectations in the younger generation that will not be tolerated in any European country.

The American model, in which economic growth is restarted, against all the odds in a mature industrial economy, by restructuring and technological innovation in an atomised labour market, is not exportable to any society with a less individualist moral and political culture. Yet it is the paradigm for policy in all conservative parties in which market liberalism is dominant. Contrary to the American neo-conservative view which market liberals in other countries have endorsed, America is not in any sense a model for a universal civilization, but rather a singularity, a limiting case, whose lessons for others are chiefly negative. The significance of the American example for older and more rooted cultures is, in fact, of a warning to be heeded rather than a model to be emulated. For in these older cultures an American model for economic policy is bound to entail far greater cultural losses, with most of the economic gains being small, speculative or entirely illusory. If there can be such a thing as a coherent form of conservative thought and policy in the European countries – and it is an implication of my argument that that is at best an open question – then it can only be one that has decoupled, economically, politically and culturally, from the American exemplar which animates the New Right.

Market liberalism, as we have come to know it in Britain and elsewhere, fosters a privileging of choice and a cult of mobility that consort badly with the settled communities cherished by traditional conservatives. Indeed, among us, market liberalism is in its workings ineluctably subversive of tradition and community. This may not have been the case in Edmund Burke's day, in which the traditions of Whig England could coexist with a policy of economic individualism, but in our age a belief in any such harmony is a snare and a delusion. Among us, unlike the men and women of Burke's day, markets are global, and also, in the case of capital markets, nearly instantaneous; free trade, if it too is global, operates among communities that are vastly more uneven in development than any that traded with one another in Burke's time; and our lives are pervaded by mass media that transform tastes and revolutionise daily habits, in ways that could be only dimly glimpsed by the Scottish political economists whom Burke so revered.

For the Scottish thinkers to whom Burke owed allegiance, there was nevertheless no pre-ordained harmony between the workings of a commercial society and the renewal of valued traditions. Adam Smith feared that the minute division of labour required in the emerging commercial society would stultify popular sensibility and intellectual development and that the anonymity of great towns would lead to a breakdown in informal social monitoring. He conjectured that the dissociation of market success from the moral virtues in commercial societies could generate a new and perverse form of emulation and that the hedonism of commercial societies would make the martial virtues unsustainable in them. As Smith himself put it, in one of his lectures on jurisprudence:

> There are some inconveniences ... arising from a commercial spirit. The first we shall mention is that it confines the views of men. Where the division of labour is brought to perfection, every man has only a simple operation to perform. To this his whole attention is confined, and few ideas pass in his mind but what have an immediate connexion with it ... Another inconvenience attending commerce is that education is greatly neglected ... we find that in the commercial parts of England, the tradesmen are for the most part in this despicable condition: their work through half the week is sufficient to maintain them, and thro' want of education they have no amusement for the other but riot and debauchery. So it may very justly be said that the people who cloath the whole world are in rags themselves ... Another bad effect of commerce is that it sinks the courage of mankind and tends to extinguish the martial

spirit. In all commercial countries the division of labour is infinite, and every ones thoughts are employed on one particular thing ... In the same manner war comes to be a trade also ... The defence of the country is therefore committed to a certain set of men who have nothing else to do; and among the bulk of the people military courage diminishes. [6]

These concerns, shared by other Scottish thinkers such as Adam Ferguson, have scarcely been shown to be groundless or exaggerated by the subsequent history of market societies. Most of Smith's latter-day epigones seem nevertheless not to have taken to heart his wise summary and conclusion:

These are the disadvantages of a commercial spirit. The minds of men are contracted and rendered incapable of elevation, education is despised or at least neglected, and heroic spirit is almost utterly extinguished. To remedy these defects would be an object worthy of serious attention. [7]

These moral and cultural shortcomings of a commercial society, so vividly captured by one of its seminal theorists, figure less prominently, if at all, in the banal discourse of free market ideology.

The social and cultural effects of market liberalism are, virtually without exception, inimical to the values that traditional conservatives hold dear. Communities are scattered to the winds by the gale of creative destruction. Endless 'downsizing' and 'flattening' of enterprises fosters ubiquitous insecurity and makes loyalty to the company a cruel joke. The celebration of consumer choice, as the only undisputed value in market societies, devalues commitment and stability in personal relationships and encourages the view of marriage and the family as vehicles of self-realisation. The dynamism of market processes dissolves social hierarchies and overturns established expectations. Status is ephemeral, trust frail and contract sovereign. The dissolution of communities promoted by market-driven labour mobility weakens, if not entirely destroys, the informal social monitoring of behaviour which is the most effective preventive measure against crime. It is odd that British conservatives, who have followed their American teachers in blaming the rise in crime in Britain on the disincentive effects of welfare measures, have not noticed that most forms of crime (apart from some sorts of property crime) are vastly commoner in the United States, where welfare institutions are far less developed, and market-driven labour mobility and its resultant *anomie* far more intense.

It is a general truth little-noted by contemporary conservatives, that the incessant change promoted and demanded by market processes nullifies the significance of precedent and destroys the authority of the past. Indeed it is not too much of an exaggeration to say that market liberal policy delivers the *coup de grâce* to practices of authority and subscription to tradition already severely weakened during the modern period. Perhaps the most salient feature of our age is not a decline in individual liberty but the vanishing of authority and a concomitant metamorphosis of moral judgements into a species of personal preferences, between which reason is powerless to arbitrate. The tendency of market liberal policy is significantly to reinforce subjectivist and even antinomian tendencies which are already very powerful in modernist societies and thereby to render surviving enclaves and remnants of traditional life powerless before them.

The Old Right project of cultural fundamentalism is best understood as an ill-thought-out response to the modern dissolution of old forms of moral life that contemporary conservative policy has itself promoted or accelerated. This is not to say that all such older forms of community and moral life lacked value. On the contrary, the reactionary perception of cultural loss as a real historical phenomenon is sometimes well-founded, and it is singularly lacking among many contemporary conservatives; but that does not mean that the old forms of life can, or even should, be reconstituted. The conservative clamour about family breakdown is not only dishonest in repressing the role that market-driven economic changes – sometimes occurring over several generations, but greatly accelerated in recent years, as with female participation in the workforce – have played in transforming family life. It is also self-deceiving in imagining that older forms of family life can conceivably be revived when modern Western demands for choice and self-fulfillment – which in other areas have a supreme and over-riding influence on conservatives – are denied. The current neo-fundamentalist clamour for a return to the traditional family is, in other words, misconceived and frivolous in the highest degree. It expresses no serious concern for the needs of people in families, nor any understanding of the diverse forms in which the institution of the family is now to be found. Such vulgar clamour is symptomatic of contemporary conservative thought in the unreality of its perception of real people and their needs. The adoption by Conservative governments of a neo-fundamentalist stance on family policy is best understood as an act of desperation, reinforced by the remoteness from public sentiment bred by the hermetic culture of the new Tory *nomenklatura*. Its political effect will be to speed Conservatives along the road to electoral oblivion.

4: The Political Economy of Erewhon: The Market Liberal Utopia

The desolation of settled communities and the ruin of established expectations will not be mourned and may well be welcomed by fundamentalist market liberals. For them, nothing much of any value is threatened by the unfettered operation of market institutions. Communities and ways of life which cannot renew themselves through the exercise of consumer choice deserve to perish. The protection from market forces of valuable cultural forms is a kind of unacceptable paternalism. And so the familiar and tedious litany goes on.

Underlying this fundamentalist conception of market institutions is a model of society that in its rationalistic utopianism and its hubristic doctrine of global convergence on a universal civilization resembles nothing more closely than the most primitive forms of classical Marxism. Classical liberalism, or what I have termed market fundamentalism, is, like Marxism, a variation on the Enlightenment project to transcend the contingencies of history and cultural difference and found a universal civilization that is qualitatively different from any that has ever before existed. The conflict between fundamentalist liberalism and the European tradition of conservative thought is plain and incontrovertible, if only in the fact that conservatives as different as Burke and de Maistre defined their outlook in terms of enmity towards the central project of the Enlightenment. It was left to the conservatives of the late twentieth century to yoke conservatism, perhaps for the first time in its history, to an Enlightenment utopia. If, as I believe, we are now in circumstances in which conservative philosophy can no longer give us much guidance, this is partly because we live in a post-Enlightenment age, an age in which the best thought regards the Enlightenment from a perspective of historical distance rather than setting itself in opposition to it. This is to say that we view the European Enlightenment, like the Renaissance and the Reformation, as a cultural transformation that has left permanent marks on all subsequent thought and practice that cannot be reversed. Equally, nor can we found policy on Enlightenment expectations – of convergence on a universal civilization, and progress in the growth of knowledge occurring in tandem with increasing human emancipation – which the historical experience of our century, and of mankind generally, renders incredible. Although it has transformed our cultures irreversibly, the Enlightenment for us - unlike for the French *philosophes*, and perhaps still for a few Old Believers in America - cannot be an ersatz religion. Our situation, as late moderns, whether we wish it or not, is to belong to a post-Enlightenment culture, in which the rationalist religions of humanity are almost as archaic, alien and remote as the traditional transcendental faiths. It is therefore deeply ironic that conservatism should have surrendered its scepticism in regard to the Enlightenment just at the historical moment when the Enlightenment project should be everywhere in evident disarray or actual collapse.

The kinship of market fundamentalism with classical

Marxism is evident in at least three respects. First, both are forms of 'economism' in that their model of man is that of *homo economicus* and they theorise cultural and political life in the reductionist terms of economic determinism. A *reductio ad absurdum* of the reductionist analysis of social life on the basis of an abstract and in fact a priori model of market exchange may be found in the works of the Chicago economist Gary Becker, but less extreme versions of the same approach are to be found in the application of economic analysis to political and bureaucratic behaviour.[8]

Second, this form of economic imperialism involves a marginalisation of cultural difference in human life that grossly underestimates its political importance and even distorts our view of market institutions. It occludes our perception of political realities by treating nationalism and ethnic allegiance as ephemeral, and even epiphenomenal or derivative, episodes in modern life. It blunts our understanding of market institutions themselves by neglecting their cultural variability – a decisive mistake at any time, but especially momentous at present, when radically different East Asian market institutions are overtaking Occidental ones, particularly the Anglo-American varieties, on virtually any measure of performance. In general, it encourages the erroneous view of market institutions as free-standing entities, and the mistaken expectation that they will converge on a single model.[9]

Third, the economic imperialism of the fundamentalist conception of market institutions suggests a view of society, explicit in Hayek and before him in Herbert Spencer, in which it is nothing but a nexus of market exchanges, such that allegiance can be secured to a liberal political order that is universal and embodies no particular cultural tradition. In this paleo-liberal or libertarian view, the erosion of distinctive cultures by market processes is, if anything, to be welcomed as a sign of progress toward a universal rational civilization. Here paleo-liberalism shows its affinities not with European conservatism but with the Old Left project of doing away with, or marginalising politically, the human inheritance of cultural difference.

It is clear that this perspective is hallucinatory and utopian if we consider its neglect of the sources not only of political allegiance but also of social order in common cultural forms. Market liberalism, like other Enlightenment ideologies, treats cultural difference as a politically marginal phenomenon whose appropriate sphere is in private life. It does not comprehend, or repudiates as irrationality, the role of a common culture in sustaining political order and in legitimating market institutions. It maintains that only a regime of common rules, perhaps embodying a shared conception of rights, is required for the stability of market institutions and a liberal civil society. This species of liberal legalism overlooks, or denies, that market institutions will not be politically stable – at any rate when they are combined with democratic institutions – if they do not accord with widespread conceptions of fairness, or violate other important cultural norms or have too destructive an effect on established expectations. In short, it denies the evident facts that the wholly free market is incompatible with social and political stability, while the stability of market institutions themselves depends far more on their political and cultural acceptability than upon the legal framework which supposedly defines and protects them.

Market liberal responses to this criticism fall into two categories: the ideological and the pragmatic. Market liberal ideologists argue that the stability of a market society is only a matter of enforcing its laws. This thoroughly foolish reply need not detain us. It neglects the political fragility of the rule of law and the frequent impossibility of enforcing it – points market liberals seem able to grasp in the context of laws which flout supply and demand, such as price controls, but which they appear incapable of generalising. The pragmatic market liberal response is to argue that market institutions need no legitimation so long as they deliver the goods in terms of general prosperity. This argument is illuminating in that it reveals the dependency of market liberal thought on the permanent possibility of rapid and continuous economic growth. It shows also that market liberalism has few sources of legitimacy on which to call when market economies go through a bad patch. It is the dim or unspoken recognition of this problem of legitimation for market institutions in times of poor economic performance that has led many market fundamentalists to compromise the rationalist purity of their doctrine and to combine it with varieties of moral or cultural fundamentalism.

Market liberalism is a utopian ideology in that the free market institutions to which it is devoted cannot be combined with social or political stability in the real world of human history. (This result is corroborated rather than undermined by the American example, in which a highly individualist ideal of market institutions has been rendered compatible with social stability only by the adoption of protectionist and regulatory policies more restrictive and far-reaching than those of almost any other Western country.) It is utopian in its view of market institutions themselves – as perpetual motion machines requiring only a legal framework and government non-interference to deliver uninterrupted growth – and in its refusal to accept that sometimes an active macro-economic policy is necessary to keep a market economy on an even keel. It is also utopian in its neglect, or denial, of the truth that market institutions are stable when, and only when, they come embedded in cultural forms which constrain and inform their workings.

Market liberalism is at its most utopian, however, in its conception of a global market society, in which goods, and perhaps people, move freely between economies of radically different stages of development and harbouring very different cultures. Global free trade, as envisaged by economic liberals and embodied in the GATT agreements of late 1993, subjects both developing and mature economies to levels of strain and job dislocation severer than they have ever known before. The displacement of peasants in hitherto agrarian economies and of industrial workers in Europe by an untrammelled global market will unavoidably have consequences for the social and political stability of both kinds of economies, that have not been addressed in the Panglossian scenarios of the supporters of world-wide free trade.[10] In Europe, the politically destabilising effects of structural unemployment in excess of 10 per cent are already visible in electoral support for renascent radical parties of the

Right. It does not need great powers of clairvoyance to divine the political impact of further large job losses arising from an influx of goods produced at around one tenth of European labour costs. Nor does it require more than a smattering of knowledge of twentieth-century history to guess the likely results of attempting to force on European peoples a structural economic adjustment larger, deeper and quicker than any they have yet suffered other than as a consequence of war. Supporters of global free trade do not confront its systemic effects on the stability of families and communities. Global free trade imposes an inexorable downward pressure on workers' incomes in the First World for a variety of reasons, including demographic ones. Further, it dislocates settled communal life by imposing unending job mobility on workers and their families. As Herman Daly has written:

> Given the existing overpopulation and high
> demographic growth of the Third World it is clear that
> equalisation [of incomes] will be downward, as it has
> indeed been during the last decade in the US ...
> Even with uniformly high wages made possible by
> universal population control and redistribution, and with
> uniform internalization of external costs, free trade and
> free capital mobility still increase the separation of
> ownership and control and the forced mobility of labour
> which are so inimical to community.[11]

These destabilising effects of global free trade are not incidental but integral to it.

The political frivolity of the utopia of a frontierless global market of the sort that is embodied in the GATT agreements is perhaps only matched by that of EU proposals that envisage a continental labour market operating under a single transnational currency. Such proposals for a deregulated single European market neglect not only the vast differences in economic development within the EU but also the embeddedness of the diverse market institutions that the EU harbours in divergent national cultures. At the same time, the project of a single European currency is bound to result in stagnant pools of unemployment, regional and even national in scope, if it is not combined with an effective transnational labour market. Such a market has no precedent in modern history and there can be little doubt that the attempt to impose it will encounter a powerful political backlash. In general, attempts to steamroller the European peoples into an artificial and culturally disembedded single market can only work to strengthen political support for nationalism. Such a reinforcement of nationalism in Europe, arising from insensitivity to national cultures, can only have the effect of making more difficult those forms of European co-operation – on a common defence and foreign policy, for example – that Europe's present circumstances make desirable and indeed urgently necessary.

Both visions, for GATT and for a federalist European Union, are neo-liberal rationalist utopias that will founder on the reefs of history and human nature, with costs in human suffering that may come to rival those of twentieth-century experiments in central economic planning. These and other similarly utopian projects of market liberalism neglect enduring needs of human beings, an understanding of which was once preserved in conservative thought. Human beings need, more than the freedom of consumer choice, a cultural and economic environment that offers them an acceptable level of security and in which they feel at home. Market institutions that deny this will be politically repudiated. The project of constructing a market liberal utopia in which these needs for security and common life are not met has as its only sure outcome the spawning of atavistic movements that wreak havoc on the historic inheritance of liberal institutions. The challenge for thought and policy is that of abandoning, once and for all, the project of any such utopia and of applying the genuine insights of conservative thought to the novel circumstances in which we find ourselves. The results of this intellectual enterprise are bound to be radical and – for many conventional Western conservatives – unacceptable.

5: What Conservatism Was

A central theme of this inquiry is that, partly because of the novelty of the times and partly because it has abandoned its most distinctive insights and concerns, conservatism is no longer a viable political outlook. Conservative thought may well not be alone in suffering obsolescence and redundancy at this juncture in history. It is plausible that both socialist thought and the standard forms of liberalism face a similar superannuation. In each of these traditions there are insights that can and should be salvaged from the wreckage, but my aim here is to identify those grains of truth in conservative thought that retain a lasting value even as conservatism itself shuffles off the scene.

As expressed by such twentieth-century writers as Oakeshott and Santayana,[12] a conservative outlook on society and government encompassed three themes that are salient to our current circumstance and which are denied, or little understood, in the presently dominant schools of free market conservatism. There is first the belief that human beings as we find them are not individual specimens of generic humanity but practitioners of particular cultures. It is from these cultures that they derive their identities, which are never that of universal humanity, but rather those conferred by the particular, and unchosen, inheritances of history and language. What is most essential about us, accordingly, is what is most accidental, and what makes each of us what he is a local and not a universal matter.[13] Indeed, in this conservative view the very meaning of anyone's life is a matter of local knowledge, and the greatest disaster that can befall any community is that the shared understandings – the myths, rituals and narratives – that confer meaning on the lives of its participants are dissipated in too rapid or too sweeping cultural change. As Oakeshott notes:

> The Masai, when they were moved from their old country to the present Masai reserve in Kenya, took with them the names of their hills and plains and rivers and gave them to the hills and plains and rivers of the new country. And it is by some such subterfuge of conservatism that every man or people compelled to suffer a notable change avoids the shame of extinction.[14]

It was by such a subterfuge that the shamanists of Lake Baikal, forbidden to worship their old gods by the Soviet communist regime, renamed them after the Paris Communards, thereby preserving from extinction both their religion and their very identity.[15]

The conservation of local knowledge, because such knowledge is constitutive of our very identity, is a central value in any outlook that is truly conservative. Local knowledge is threatened, or destroyed, by economic or cultural changes that are large and incessant. It is by now recognised that agricultural collectivisation in Soviet Russia and the Ukraine resulted not only in millions of deaths but in a loss of the practical knowledge of farmers and a destruction of peasant cultural traditions that are irreversible. Less commonly perceived is the loss of local knowledge that comes about through constant business reorganisation, ephemeral job tenure and unremitting mobility of labour, which are forced on contemporary societies by unrestricted market competition. There is a real paradox here, one that has gone wholly unremarked in the banal discourse of recent conservatism, in that the epistemic argument for market institutions, which rightly stresses their superiority over planning institutions in utilising dispersed local knowledge, must be supplemented by the observation that unfettered markets tend to destroy or dissipate local knowledge. They do so by rendering local knowledge increasingly obsolete or irrelevant to the operation of market processes that are themselves ever more disembedded. If, as I am inclined to think, conservatism is best stated not as a moral but as an epistemic doctrine – as the doctrine that the knowledge that is most important in the lives of human beings is local, practical, traditional and, as Edward Goldsmith has reminded us, ineffable[16] – then contemporary conservatism founders on the contradiction that it has committed itself to the hegemony of market institutions whose workings render traditional human knowledge worthless and the social world unintelligible in its terms.

A fundamental objection to the paleo-liberal regime of incessant economic change under unfettered market institutions, then, is that in devaluing traditional knowledge it renders social and economic life ever less understandable to its human participants. In so doing, unfettered market institutions tend to deplete the cultural identities of their practitioners – upon which these institutions themselves depend. Market institutions will enhance human well-being and will be stably renewed across the generations, when they do not go against the grain of the particular cultures that harbour them, but on the contrary assist those cultures to reproduce themselves. By imposing on people a regime of incessant change and permanent revolution, unencumbered market institutions deplete the stock of historical memory on which cultural identity depends. The cliché that globalised markets tend to yield cultural uniformity is therefore not without an element of truth. What such cultural homogenisation signifies is perhaps less obvious: a breach in historical memory which disrupts, or empties of significance, the narratives in terms of which people make sense of their lives. If, as any conservative who is also a sceptic is bound to think, the meaning of life for all of us is a local matter, this junking of local knowledge by unencumbered market processes is no small matter. For these and similar reasons, the loss of historical memory brought about by globalised market forces will be recognised – on any view that is authentically conservative, or for that matter reflectively liberal – as a form of cultural impoverishment, not a stage on the way to a universal civilization. Let us call this first conservative belief 'anti-universalism', which is the insight that cultural difference belongs to the human essence, and its concomitant, the perception that the identities of human beings depend on the renewal of the particular cultural forms by which they are constituted.

A second conservative theme is what I shall call 'non-progress', or anti-meliorism. By this I mean the conservative rejection of the idea of indefinite world-improvement as either a realistic or a desirable end of political life. It is common among conservative thinkers to stress the Augustinian insight that, like all things human, political institutions are imperfect and imperfectible, so that the project of a 'political providence' which promises to deliver mankind from mystery and tragedy – which was the project of Marxism-Leninism – is at once impious (from the standpoint of any religious believer) and impossible. The perception of human imperfectibility is, however, only one reason, and perhaps not in the end the most important, why a conservative will reject the idea of progress, at least as an animating idea in political and economic life. He will reject it because it presupposes a uniform standard of evaluation and improvement of human life, whereas it is an implication of his first belief that, limiting cases aside, such standards will vary across different cultures. If the bottom line in political and moral reasoning is a conception of human well-being, and if human well-being is bound up with participation in common cultural forms whose content varies to a significant degree, then there will, except in limiting cases, be no common measure for improvement in different cultures. It is not then the possibility of global betterment that the conservative rejects so much as its meaningfulness.

For a conservative there is surely something anomalous in making progress, rather than the sustainability or stability of society, the end of political life. Any decent society will do what it can to alleviate the unavoidable misfortunes of human life, to enable and empower its members in coping with them and to ensure those that cannot be avoided can nevertheless be borne with dignity and consolation. The politics of open-ended improvement, however, was, and is – or should be – alien to a conservative sensibility. Such a melioristic approach to human life cannot help encouraging unreal hopes of the human future and distracting us from dealing with the minute particulars of our lives as they are now. As Santayana comments:

> We all feel at this time the ambiguity of mechanical progress. It seems to multiply opportunity, but it destroys the possibility of simple, rural or independent life. It lavishes information, but it abolishes mastery except in trivial or mechanical efficiency. We learn many languages, but we degrade our own. Our philosophy is highly critical and thinks itself enlightened, but it is a Babel of mutually unintelligible artificial tongues.[17]

And the idea of indefinite progress is easily associated with the notion that social dilemmas are soluble by the generation of ever more resources through economic growth. This association is not a necessary or inevitable one, as we can see from the example of John Stuart Mill, who insisted that a stationary state need not be one in which human improvement has come to a halt.[18] But it is a common one which contemporary conservative thought does nothing to question. The fact is that in conservative thought, as we know it today, a vulgar and unreflective meliorism about the human prospect is combined with a crudely economistic conception of what social improvement consists in. It is not from this thin gruel that we can hope for sustenance.

The third element in a conservative outlook I shall call 'the primacy of cultural forms', or anti-reductionism. By this I mean the idea, implied by much that has gone before, that neither market institutions nor political institutions can or should be autonomous in regard to the cultures they serve. Rather, they are themselves to be assessed, and controlled, by reference to the ends and norms of the cultures in which they are embedded. Market institutions which have been disembedded from their underlying cultures may increase the output of goods and services but they will not enhance human well-being through their activities.[19] Again the idea that there is, or could be, a single model for market institutions is to be rejected, since they will properly vary according to their cultural matrices and social contexts. In this conservative view, the disembedding of market institutions from their parent cultures, and the conferring on them of functional autonomy, is one of the disasters of modern societies since it amounts to a severance of markets from the ends they appropriately serve. The denial of the primacy of cultural forms is, of course, an implication of any neo-liberal view that makes a fetish of consumer choice, and of any more developed liberal philosophy which accords an intrinsic value to choice-making independent of the goodness of that which is chosen. And it is a necessary presupposition of the knee-jerk response of economic liberals which regards all political intervention in economic life as an evil that stands in need of justification.

The deeper import of the idea of the primacy of cultural forms is that it is not through the activity of choice-making that values are created in our lives. The conception of the autonomous human subject, though it is a central one in contemporary liberal thought, and one which I have myself deployed in an earlier work,[20] easily degenerates into a dangerous fiction. In its common uses, the idea of autonomy neglects the central role in human life of chance and fate – of the unchosen accidents that confer our identities on us and the further accidents that befall us that choice has no part in and, where they are misfortunes, can do little or nothing to remedy. And it sanctifies that fiction of liberal philosophy, the fiction of the unsituated human subject, which is author of its ends and creator of the values in its life. It is, indeed, this liberal fiction whose emaciated ghost stalks the dim ruins of paleo-liberal ideology, gibbering of global markets and economic efficiency.

In the subtlest liberal uses of the idea of autonomy, it is recognised that the exercise of autonomous choice depends for its value on a cultural environment that is rich in choiceworthy options and inherently public goods.[21] In this subtler liberal perspective, value is not an artefact of individual choice, it is discovered rather than created by us, and what has value in our lives is often far from transparent to us.[22] It is arguable, and plausible, that even this subtler liberal conception of autonomy unreasonably privileges a particular Western ideal, whose costs and illusions it has not fully perceived.[23] From the standpoint being developed in this paper, the ideal of autonomy has the clear danger of reinforcing the excesses of individualism promoted in neo-liberal thought and policy by further undervaluing the human need for common forms of life. All that is of value in the subtler liberal conception of autonomy can be captured, without the excesses of individualism, in the ideas of independence and enablement, where the human subjects that are so enabled are not the fictions of liberal theory but

45

flesh and blood practitioners of particular, historically constituted forms of life. It is with the enablement of human beings as they are in the real world of history and practice, embedded in their specific and diverse cultures, traditions and communities, rather than with the rights of the empty ciphers of liberal theory, that political thought and public policy ought rightly to be concerned. Such concerns are only obfuscated by the shallow discourse of choice and rights that has dominated British life for the last decade and more.

6: After Conservatism

The conservative idea of the primacy of cultural forms is meant to displace not only standard liberal conceptions of the autonomous human subject but also ideas of the autonomy of market institutions that liberal thought has recently been applied – or misapplied – to support. It is not meant to support paleo-conservative and reactionary conceptions of organic or integral community which have no application in our historical circumstances and which, if they were implemented politically, could end only in tragedy or – more likely in Britain – black comedy. The idea of a seamless community – the 'noumenal community', as we may call it, of recent communitarianism[24] – is as much of a fiction as the autonomous subject of liberal theory. We all of us belong to many communities, we mostly inherit diverse ethnicities, and our world-views are fractured and provisional whether or not we know or admit it. We harbour a deep diversity of views and values regarding sexuality and the worth of human life, our relations with the natural environment and the special place, if any, of the human species in the scheme of things. The reactionary project of rolling back this diversity of values and world-views in the pursuit of a lost cultural unity[25] overlooks the character of our cultural inheritance as a palimpsest, having ever deeper layers of complexity.

Those who imagine that diversity and uncertainty of world-view are confined to the chattering classes are themselves captivated by the constructions of their own discourse. The healthy, unreflective folk culture of their imagination corresponds to nothing in common life; and the assertion of robust common sense against the depredations of 'theorists' and opinion formers is itself made ridiculous by the bookish ignorance it displays. Among us, High Toryism can only be a pose, a playful or frivolous distraction from serious political reflection in a world in which authority and tradition are barely memories. For us a common culture cannot – and, for anyone touched by a liberal sensibility, should not – be a seamless web. It must consist of what the diverse traditions that our society harbours can recognise as a shared inheritance, which will reasonably change over time. The liberal legalist view and the reactionary or organicist view are equally removed from the realities and needs of our current circumstances. The effect of market liberalism has been to run down our common stock of cultural traditions by propagating the absurd liberal legalist view that we do not need a common culture only common rules, while the patent failings of this paleo-liberal view have inspired the vain attempt to recapture a lost cultural unity. Cultural fundamentalism has emerged in a vain attempt to shore up the tottering edifice of market fundamentalism. Neither conservative position seriously answers to our present needs.

In Part II of this book David Willetts, in the most appealing and persuasive defence of a contemporary conservative view – somewhat distinct from any reactionary or organicist posture – argues that the disruptive effects of unfettered market institutions on the lives of communities have been much exaggerated. It is probably not an unfair caricature of this position to say that it is confident that in conditions of steady economic growth communities are pretty robust and can in most things safely be left to their own devices. It is hard to see what in contemporary conditions justifies such confidence. It may be true that communities were able to renew themselves in circumstances of rapid economic change in England in the latter part of the nineteenth century, say, but such circumstances cannot be replicated now. At that time, much of the English working class was subject to the influence of nonconformist Christianity, with all the restraints on behaviour that that implied, including a form of family life in which duty and commitment had priority over self-realisation and romantic love. Personal behaviour was subject to a level of social monitoring, to norms of respectability and to sanctions of ostracism and stigma that are unknown among us today. Neighbourhoods and churches were small, slow-moving to face societies in which such sanctions were real and telling. None of these conditions stands in Britain today or will exist in any realistically foreseeable future. They have been destroyed by a century and more of social changes which market liberal policies have only accelerated and deepened. Most of Britain is a post-religious, and in particular a post-Christian society, for good or ill, and the culture of marriage and the family is permeated by ideals of choice and self-fulfilment of the sorts celebrated by latter-day defenders of the free market. And, as I have noted, the fragmentation of family life which contemporary conservatives bemoan is, in very large part, a product of the culture of choice and the economy of unrestricted mobility, which they themselves celebrate.

It may be that the best prospects for traditional

conservative values are to be found today not in any Occidental country but in the East Asian cultures. The absence, or weakness, in these cultures of the romantic and individualist conception of married life that characterises Western bourgeois societies, and which are at their strongest in those societies, for example in America, where family breakdown is most pervasive and extreme, may well go a long way toward accounting for their extraordinary economic achievements. It is ironical that the East Asian societies, which have been more successful than most Occidental countries in combining dynamic market institutions with stable communities, should have been so little studied by Western conservatives. No-one imagines that the successes of East Asian countries can be replicated in the very different cultural and historical milieux in which we find ourselves in Europe today. It is nevertheless a reflection on the poverty of Western conservatism that it should have failed to reflect on the experience of countries that have been more successful than any Western country in finding and maintaining the elusive balance between the claims of individual choice and the human need for a life in common.

For us, in Britain today, individualism and pluralism are a historical fate. We may reasonably hope to temper this fate, and thereby to make the best of the opportunities it offers us: we cannot hope to escape it. Yet it is just such an escape from our historical fate that is promised by those conservatives who seek answers to our social problems in the revival of religious and moral beliefs and disciplines – 'Victorian values' – that vanished generations ago. It is idle and silly to imagine that the resources of self-discipline, or the forms of social monitoring, exist among us now which sustained the deferral of gratification among the mid-Victorians. The close neighbourhoods of Victorian times have been dissolved by the demands of labour mobility. Family life has changed utterly with contraception and the increased, and sometimes predominant role of married women in the provision of the family income. Nor are these changes necessarily, or in fact, by any means all for the bad. The point is that they remove many of the resources whereby mid-nineteenth century communities renewed themselves in the face of rapid economic change. It is hard to understand the confidence of those who believe that communities without these resources will succeed in adapting to the impact of economic changes powered by far greater, and far more swiftly moving, global market forces.

Such confidence arises, in all probability, from a failure to perceive that the requirements of unfettered market institutions and those of stable communities may and do come into deep conflict. It expresses also, no doubt, resistance to the policy implication of such a perception, which is that communities need shelter from the gale of market competition, else they will be scattered to the winds. In the last resort, this contemporary conservative view regards communities as adjuncts to markets, optional extras in a society of market exchanges, rather than the sources of the needs markets exist to serve. It can therefore never accept that markets may need to be constrained, or channelled, so as to meet the needs of communities. For constraints on markets will presumably entail losses of efficiency, and so of output. And any loss of output, particularly if it is produced by political intervention aiming to protect something as elusive as the stability of a community, must be an error in policy. This contemporary conservative view is in the end, accordingly, a variation on a familiar theme of market liberalism, which is that market institutions are justified as engines of economic growth. My argument, however, is that – as Aristotle observed – economic activity is senseless unless it satisfies human needs. It is this old and homely truth that the new conservatism, even in its most intelligent forms, seems to have determinedly forgotten.

7: New Measures for Conserving Common Life

All strands of conventional political and economic thought are at one in staking our future on a continuation of economic growth as we have hitherto known it. They all thereby commit themselves to a political version of Pascal's wager – itself a notoriously bad bet. It would seem more prudent to think and plan on the assumption that the common fate of the mature economies – the economies of Western Europe and Japan, for example – is low economic growth, and to begin to consider how social and political life may best be organised when – doubtless willy-nilly rather than by any kind of premeditated policy – we find ourselves landed in something akin to a stationary state economy. The problems of legitimating market institutions in a context in which no-one can expect his or her income or living standards to rise automatically, have as yet hardly begun to be discussed.

The dilemmas opened up by the prospect of a near-stationary economy are not only political. The promise of an open horizon of growth and an indefinite improvement in the human lot have served as a surrogate for religious conviction in an age in which the great *political* fact is the passing of Christianity. An inexorable consequence of the passing of Christianity – understood here not as a variety of personal faith but as the unifying world-view of a culture – is the waning of the secular religions of progress and humanity in which Christian moral hopes found political expression. The cultural void that yawns when the secular meliorism of the religion of growth founders, is as yet too far away to be on any intellectual or political agenda. If it is thought of at all, it is as an element in a fundamentalist project for the rechristianisation of Western societies which can be taken seriously by no one with any sense of historical perspective. The question of what is to be the content of the common culture in a country such as Britain, when it is no longer animated by inherited transcendental faith or by any variety of the Enlightenment project, is a deep and difficult one that I cannot consider here. It is clear only that, for us at any rate, a common culture cannot mean a common world-view, religious or secular. It is an implication of all that I have said, however, that we have no option but to struggle to make our inheritance of liberal traditions work. At present, the principal obstacle we face in the struggle to renew our inheritance of liberal practice is the burden on thought and policy of market liberal dogma.

Liberal dogmas work to occlude our perception of the dangers to liberal society arising from current policies. They dim our vision, most particularly, of the dangers to social and political stability arising from the ever greater autonomy of market institutions. Little serious thought has yet been given, for example, to the problems arising from the combination of a near stationary state economy with rapidly ongoing technological innovation which market institutions are producing in most, if not all, of the world's mature economies. This is a combination whose difficulties John Stuart Mill, writing on the stationary state in the mid-nineteenth century, could hardly be expected to anticipate. The central difficulty is that the enlargement of leisure that

Mill, by contrast with the gloomier classical economists, expected to come from stability in population and output against a background of improvement in the industrial arts is occurring in the form of ever higher levels of involuntary unemployment. There can be little doubt that for the medium to longer term the agenda to consider is that of redefining full employment as a policy objective in terms that do not mean full-time jobs in an expanding economy. It may be that proposals for a basic or citizen's income, where that is to be distinguished from the neo-liberal idea of a negative income tax, and a better distribution of capital among the citizenry, need reconsideration – despite all their difficulties – as elements in a policy aiming to reconcile the human need for economic security with the destabilising dynamism of market institutions.[26] Even the outlines of a policy for such a new pattern of full employment, however, are as yet barely visible to us.

We can nevertheless be reasonably sure that the difficult transition to this new order of things will be made impossible if the relentless elimination of jobs by advances in technology is compounded by the job-destroying effects in the mature economies of global free trade. The proposition that Western labour forces can or must adapt to a global labour market in which their competitors earn a tenth of their wages is not one that commends itself either to good sense or political prudence. Nor is global free trade forced on us by anything in the Ricardian theory of comparative advantage, since a regional free trade area such as the EEA is already larger than any that has ever before existed in human history and is diverse enough to satisfy all the Ricardian requirements. Indeed it is far from clear that Ricardian theory demands, or even supports, global free trade. Ricardo himself had doubts about the idea of comparative advantage, especially when it involves the technology-driven displacement of labour, that seem to have eluded his latter-day disciples. In his *Principles of Political Economy and Taxation* in a chapter entitled ' On Machinery', Ricardo states, 'I am convinced that the substitution of machinery for human labour is often very injurious to the interests of the class of labourers.' He goes on to write:

> the discovery and use of machinery may be attended with a diminution of gross produce; and whenever that is the case, it will be injurious to the labouring class, as some of their number will be thrown out of employment, and population will become redundant compared with the funds which are to employ it.

He concludes:

> the opinion entertained by the labouring class, that the employment of machinery is frequently detrimental to their interests, is not founded on prejudice and error, but is conformable to the correct principles of political economy. [27]

It is fair to surmise that the force of Ricardo's doubts could only have been increased in a circumstance, such as ours, when an untramelled global market in labour-saving technologies is envisaged and on the way to being implementated through the GATT agreements. It is, indeed, just such a circumstance – in which employers make productivity and profitability gains at the cost of unemployment and reduced incomes for workers – that Ricardo envisaged. For his followers, by contrast, the benefits of free trade are a priori truths, which mere observation cannot hope to bring into question.

On presently observable evidence, the likely result of the GATT agreements, if they are ever implemented, is not only ruin for Third World agriculture, with a billion or more peasants being displaced from the land in the space of a generation or less, but – as Sir James Goldsmith warned [28] – class war in the advanced countries as wages fall and the return on offshore capital rises. It defies both common sense and historical experience to suppose that the economic and social dislocations produced by exposure to a global market larger, more dynamic and more uneven in development than any that has ever before existed, can be absorbed by reductions in wages and shifts of manpower on a scale and at a rate that are wholly unprecedented, without a political backlash emerging in response to the devastating impact of this process of structural adjustment on working-class living standards. Such a backlash is made all the more likely given that this adjustment is demanded of working people at precisely the time when much of the social protection embodied in the post-war welfare state is being dismantled. In this historical context, global free trade is a recipe for social conflict and political instability on a large scale. A prerequisite for any policy that can hope to offer a decent measure of economic security to the population is accordingly an urgent reconsideration of the market liberal dogma of unregulated global free trade.

Market liberal policy is harmful to settled communities in many other areas. Policy in regard to cities has in Britain been grotesquely poor, with their deformation as communities by the private motor car, and their hollowing out by such developments as warehouse shopping being particularly unacceptable examples. Here the culprit is not primarily the influence of special interests, important though that undoubtedly has been, but rather neo-liberal blindness to the city itself as an institution and a form of life that is worthy of preservation and renewal. Cities – at least as these have been understood hitherto in the European tradition to which Britain belongs – are not congeries of strangers. They are not nomadic encampments, traffic islands or ephemeral aggregates of enterprises and households. They are long-standing human settlements, spanning the generations, whose welfare can neither be understood nor assured as an upshot of a myriad of uncoordinated private decisions. Protecting cities as human settlements demands institutions for accountability and planning, devolved as far as is feasible and appropriate, which are anathema to neo-liberal dogma. This is only one example, but a vitally important one, of the way in which conservative policy cast in a neo-liberal mould has been inimical to the conservation of precious cultural achievements and forms of common life.

It is not my intention to try and address here the whole range of policy issues in which market liberal thinking has led conservatives astray.[29] The key alterations in conservative thought that must precede any such detailed re-examination of policy are scrapping the conception of market institutions as perpetual motion machines for economic growth and abandoning indefinite growth in output as a sensible objective of human effort. This is not to say that as an objective growth must be replaced by no growth. That would be hardly less nonsensical, since economic growth is itself a statistical abstraction that takes no account of the contribution to human well-being of the activities it purportedly measures. What it means rather is that economic activity is not an end in itself but must serve the needs and values of the cultures in which it is pursued. It must be sustainable in its longer-term impact on both the natural and the human environments, at least in the weak sense that it does not result in their irreversible degradation. And it must be sustainable in the stronger sense that it fosters, instead of undermining, stability in the communities it affects. Of course, stability is not fixity, and we cannot put the genie of technological virtuosity back into the bottle. But this is only to say that economic change is continuous and unavoidable and must therefore be channelled, not that it can be let to run its course with the devil taking the hindmost.

Such channelling of unavoidable economic change is unlikely to be successful so long as public policy and indeed the public culture are animated by the idea of the insatiability of ever-expanding human wants. I have argued elsewhere that a conception of satiable human needs has a central role in reasoned discourse about public policy.[30] The idea of a satiable human need will be workable in public discourse, however, only if the ruling ideal of the unending proliferation of human wants is relinquished and replaced by a conception of *sufficiency* in which it is the quality of social life, rather than the quantity of goods and services, that is the central objective of public policy. One of my themes in this book is that political parties in Britain and similar countries have been slow to recognise that, in conditions of low economic growth, political discourse is bound to focus increasingly on quality-of-life issues. A connected point is that, once we no longer expect or hope for a resumption of economic growth that can allow a return to full employment as has conventionally been understood, we are free to consider how new forms of livelihood can be developed to supplement, or replace, older forms of job-holding. What is particularly important to note here is that the pursuit of sufficiency, in the context of providing people with opportunities for fulfilling livelihoods and elsewhere, presupposes that market institutions be subject to political constraints. We have no hope of achieving fulfilling livelihoods for all in the context of technology-driven displacement of labour by global free trade. The content of sufficiency, for any particular society at any particular time, must be a political judgement, arrived at by reasoned public discourse. Equally, the pursuit of sufficiency requires public policies in which the autonomy of market institutions is subordinated to political objectives of social stability and harmonious community.

Nothing advanced here is meant to cast doubt on the centrality and indispensability of market institutions in economic life. The point is that they must be harnessed and guided by political constraints if they are to serve human needs. Provided this condition is met, market institutions may well be extended in some areas of policy, where such extension helps to anchor institutions in local communities. There remains a good case for educational vouchers, not on the neo-liberal ground of promoting market competition, but on the ground that sensibly designed voucher schemes might render schools more sensitive than they are now to families and communities. Drawing on the ideas of Ivan Illich rather than upon neo-liberal thought, I have elsewhere advanced a version of an educational credit scheme which is not tied to any particular form of schooling and can be used by a diversity of institutions, traditions and communities.[31] A streamlined, or minimalist National Curriculum, could provide a common core of skills and knowledge as a standard for all families to meet, while they were otherwise free to meet the varying needs of their different communities. The details of such an educational credit scheme are less important than its objective, which is to harness market institutions to anchor schools, and other educational institutions, more securely in the communities they exist to serve. In some areas of welfare policy, also, voucher schemes can be defended as devices for devolving welfare institutions to the level closest to individuals, families and their communities. There are doubtless other, similar ways in which market institutions can be usefully extended. Such extension must always have the aim of embedding markets in the communities they serve and it must never concede to markets the autonomy and freedom from political constraint by which they have been privileged in neo-liberal theory.

8: The Prospects

The conquest of conservative parties by neo-liberal ideology, and the embodiment of that ideology in public policy, have irreversibly altered the social and political landscape of countries such as Britain. In delegitimating traditional institutions, and confounding the expectations on which the lives of Conservative voters of all classes – but especially the middle classes – were based, neo-liberal policy has all but destroyed the social base of conservatism in Britain. A secular conservatism devoted to the protection of voters' economic interests – the only remotely plausible conservatism in a post-religious country such as Britain – has been taken off the political agenda for the foreseeable future by Tory policies which have ravaged and almost destroyed the traditional economic constituencies of British conservatism. This undoing of conservatism by market liberalism is now an established fact of political life in Britain and in similarly placed countries. The likelihood that it has caused prolonged periods of electoral defeat for conservative governments and parties is, from the perspective of the present inquiry, less important than the exhaustion it betokens in conservative thought itself. The return of Conservatives to government at some time in the future, due to contingencies we cannot presently foresee, is a possibility that cannot definitively be excluded. Unlike the crazed neo-liberal ideologues of the 1980s, who pronounced that 'Labour will never rule again', we must never forget the phenomenon of chance in political life – the permanent political relevance of Cleopatra's nose – or neglect the related phenomenon of apparently deep-seated trends suddenly, and unpredictably, reversing themselves.

If, as I imagine, the Conservatives now face a long period of political marginality in Britain, conceivably lasting a generation, it could nevertheless be foreshortened considerably by errors and misfortunes occurring during a time of rule by the parties of the Left. It remains thoroughly unclear, however, what, if anything, a Conservative government arising from failures in government on the Left would be devoted to conserving. The paradoxical likelihood is that – in Britain at any rate – the task of conserving, perhaps in altered forms, the best elements in our institutional inheritance will pass to parties which presently think of themselves as being on the Left. If supposed conservatives succumb to the pseudo-radicalism of free market ideology, then genuine conservatives have no option but to become true radicals. And, if ordinary people cannot find in the party of the Right concern for their security from crime, economic risk and the breakdown of community, they will turn elsewhere for it. In so doing they will only be giving electoral expression to what has long been a fact – that conservatism in Britain has lost any clear perception of what it is that ordinary people are most concerned to protect in their lives. It is the demise of any recognisable Tory philosophy, far more than the fatigue and loss of the will to rule produced by too long a spell in power, that best explains the electoral rout currently facing British conservatism.

What 'Left' and 'Right' may mean in the coming years, and whether these terms will retain much usefulness, is not yet clear. What is unmistakably clear is that the intellectual hegemony in political life of the Right, as we used to understand it, is over. Moreover, it has become evident that conservative thought, lacking the intellectual resources needed to cope with the dilemmas thrown up by the conservative policies of the past decade or so, has in effect created the conditions for its own demise. Neither the conservative denial that the conflict between unfettered market institutions and stable communities is real, nor the reactionary project of recovering a vanished past, are sustainable responses to our predicament. Both, in their different ways, evade the real challenge of the post-socialist age, which is that of harnessing market institutions to the needs of stable communities and so giving liberal civilization another lease on life.

The evident debility of conservative thought is only one sign of the obsolescence of the principal Western ideologies, which is mirrored in the ongoing melt-down, virtually world-wide, of the political and economic models which they sponsor. My focus here has been on the specious claims of paleo-liberal ideology, in which individual choice is elevated to the supreme value and at the same time emptied of all moral significance. Our present situation is the awkward one in which we can renew and extend liberal civilization only insofar as we recognise its embeddedness in common forms of life unrecognised in liberal theory. It is unlikely that we will succeed in giving liberal society another lease of life if our intellectual outlook does not become – at least by the standards of recent liberal theorising – post-liberal. Within liberal thought, as within conservative thought, there are doubtless insights and truths that will survive the wreckage of liberal ideology; but the ruin of liberalism as an ideology is an undeniable fact of our present predicament. To the extent that as we accept this fact and thereby adopt a post-liberal perspective, we are bound to reject all those varieties of conservatism in which fundamentalist liberalism has found a political home.

An appropriate response to our present circumstance is a strategy of salvage and retrieval, of the kind attempted here with respect to the insights that have survived the wreckage of conservative philosophy. We will cope best with the new dilemmas we confront if we accept the undoing of conservatism and learn the lessons its undoing has to teach us. We may then be able to summon up the readiness to think afresh about a world in which conservative thought no longer gives us guidance or illumination.

Part II:
Civic Conservatism

9: The Problem Stated

The roots of the difficulties encountered by the last government were not to be found in the last recession, nor indiscipline by the Parliamentary Party, nor any mistakes made by the government itself. The problem was much deeper and ultimately an intellectual one. It was a dangerous uncertainty about the nature of modern conservatism.

Sometimes this thought is expressed by the observation that Conservatives have slain so many dragons – trade union barons, nationalised industries, the Soviet Empire – that we are left without a purpose: victims of our own success. It is as if Conservatives have worked themselves out of a job. But there are still enormous political challenges to face – from strengthening the supply-side of the economy, through addressing the problems of crime and incivility to raising education standards. To that list could be added those battles which are never over and test the mettle of any government, such as containing the costs of the welfare state and cutting public expenditure. The free market remains relevant to all these issues, but we are not as confident about this as we once were.

The real problem is that conservatives have become wary of relying as heavily on the free market as they appeared to do in the 1980s. It was Marx who first observed that in modern capitalism all relationships became 'commodified'; they all became market transactions. There are many good conservatives who must now be regarded as sharing this Marxist critique. Their feeling is not that the government is doing too little, but that it is doing too much. They fear that nothing is to be safe from this market reductionism, be it in the form of market testing, the internal market or ever more ambitious privatisations. Contract culture appears to have triumphed and the accountants rule: a situation that leaves many traditional conservatives uneasy.

Looking back on the passionate disputes which have dominated the Conservative Party over recent years, two crucial issues stand out. The first of course is Europe and the future of the nation state, which is under pressure as much from the global economy and the logic of the single market as the designs of the federalists. The second issue, which lies behind the Back to Basics campaign and the concern about incivility and declining standards of behaviour, single parents and juvenile crime, is the future of the family. The family is under pressure from changes in the labour market and ever greater mobility, as well as from the explicit anti-family agenda of some. There is a connection between these two issues: the nation state and the family are the two most significant non-market institutions. They have aroused such passion and confusion because Conservatives believe they cannot be reduced to the imperatives of the market-place: hence the vigour with which they have leapt to their defence even whilst the 'realists' wonder if the battle can be won and the cynics observe that the real enemy is the free market which the Conservative Party has unleashed. No wonder these arguments leave conservatives feeling a mixture of defiance, alarm and self-doubt. My purpose in this book is to show how these uncertainties might be dispelled. This involves keeping the free market at the heart of conservatism whilst showing how it is compatible with strengthening those institutions and values which can never be reduced to market transactions.

Whenever conservatives try to draw attention to a social issue, to talk about their shared values and traditions, indeed, whenever they try to talk about anything in politics which goes beyond what would be found in a company's annual report, the critics gleefully pounce: 'you cannot appeal to any sense of community, you cannot talk about values because the biggest threat to these values comes from the free markets which you have unleashed'. As free marketeers, it seems conservatives are condemned to talk only about profit and loss, not right and wrong. Conservatives need to tackle head on this crucial challenge that markets undermine values, that commerce destroys culture. It is a challenge which touches a particular chord with British conservatives precisely because the Conservative Party is so long-lived, so intertwined with Britain's history, traditions and institutions. Turning round and accusing conservatism of destroying them by unleashing free markets is painfully perverse.

The argument is often presented as a striking new criticism of the way in which the Conservative Party has developed in the last twenty years but really it has been a theme in British political debate for at least two centuries. Thomas Carlyle denounced what he called 'the Gospel of Mammon' 150 years ago:

> We call it a Society; and go about professing openly the totalest separation, isolation. Our life is not a mutual helpfulness; but rather, cloaked under due laws-of-war, named 'fair competition' and so forth, it is a mutual

hostility. We have profoundly forgotten everywhere that *Cash-payment* is not the sole relation of human beings.[32]

The argument is not merely that free markets are unpleasant, but that they are also pernicious. They are supposed to spread a way of thinking, the market way of thinking, which destroys other values including, ironically, values which capitalism itself needs to thrive. Joseph Schumpeter writing fifty years ago is perhaps the most distinguished exponent of this view:

> Capitalism creates a critical frame of mind which, after having destroyed the moral authority of so many other institutions, in the end turns against its own; the bourgeois finds to his amazement that the rationalist attack does not stop at the credentials of kings and popes, but goes on to attack private property and the whole scheme of bourgeois values. The bourgeois fortress thus becomes politically defenceless.[33]

This is what he believed to be the real internal contradiction of capitalism: it would collapse not, as Marxists wrongly predicted, because the workers became even poorer, but paradoxically because of its own success. It would destroy the very values – deferred gratification, self discipline, respect for promises and contracts – that were necessary to sustain it. Today's leader writers who attribute all our social ills to the evil effects of a philosophy which they say is just 'Me and Here and Now' are thus placing themselves in a long tradition of denunciations of the market.

Some conservatives are inclined to reply by playing down the role of the market in conservative thought, but this is bad history. Edmund Burke went into politics as a follower of Adam Smith and free markets have been at the centre of conservatism ever since. Nevertheless there is more to conservatism than this.

Conservatism is at its finest and its most distinctive precisely when it integrates a commitment to the free market into the core values and institutions which hold our country together. How conservatives might achieve such a reconciliation will be my theme in this book.

10: Understanding Our History

To understand the role of markets in conservatism, we also have to understand their role in Britain's history. There are still people who believe the caricature that free markets were discovered by Milton Friedman and imported to Britain by Keith Joseph and Mrs Thatcher in the late 1970s, like some nasty foreign predator recklessly let loose in our country and destroying our indigenous species. This failure to understand our own history helps explain the tendency for political debate to be distorted by misplaced fears of the damage which the free market might do our traditional institutions.

The historical truth is not just that Britain is a free market society but that it was the first market society. Alan Macfarlane's classic study, *The Origins of English Individualism*, offers a fascinating account of England before the Industrial Revolution. He shows that, unlike the Continent, England never experienced the classic medieval social order: there were no English serfs. Free men were selling their labour and exchanging land all through the Middle Ages, and when, at the Stuart Restoration, leasehold under the Crown was converted to freehold, it was the final recognition of a long established reality.[34] To believe that Britain underwent the Industrial Revolution and then became a free market economy is to misunderstand the historical process. Britain, rather, was the first free market society and was thus ripe for the Industrial Revolution.

A piece of evidence in support of this interpretation, directly relevant to today's policy arguments about the environment, is the network of property rights in the countryside. American environmentalists have now recognised that one of their greatest problems is that much of the Midwest belongs to the federal government and does not have enlightened owners concerned to maintain the value of their property. They look with envy at the intricate network of property rights established in England by the end of the Middle Ages – fishing rights, hunting rights, laws of trespass and laws about the use of common land. The beauty of the English countryside is a testament to the work of centuries of inherited property rights. By contrast, as Alice Coleman has shown, the desolation and alienation of an inner city estate is a direct consequence of the lack of clear property rights.[35]

When Adam Smith wrote *The Wealth of Nations* he was challenging a contemporary economic doctrine – mercantilism – but his own insights matched Britain's historical experience over previous centuries. That may help explain why his ideas were absorbed so easily by what was to become the Conservative Party. Edmund Burke, the High Tory, was the author of the free market *Notes on Scarcity* and the advocate of what he called 'economical reform' to eliminate waste in the public sector. Adam Smith famously observed of Edmund Burke that 'he was the only man who, without communication, thought on these topics exactly as he did'. Pitt the Younger, Liverpool and Peel pursued a policy of free trade, tax-cutting, deregulation and tight monetary control that would now be called monetarism. This project was part of sweeping away the old patronage style politics of the eighteenth century and creating instead a model of limited government. The high moral tone of

Victorian politics was not achieved by accident – it was a direct consequence of the success of the free market project in reshaping British institutions in the first half of the nineteenth century. The 'Old Corruption' was associated with heavy government involvement in the economy; free market reforms did not just strengthen the economy but also raised the tone of political debate.

As politicians wrestle today with the problems of urban incivility, shiftless young men and a sense that powerful economic forces are wrenching apart an established social order, we should remember that the Victorians went through similarly dramatic changes. They experienced rapid industrialisation, the biggest population movements in our history, the emergence of enormous new cities together with a population boom that gave Victorian society an age profile as youthful as in the Third World today. They saw themselves as 'shooting the rapids' – on the other side of which was a civil and democratic society in which everyone participated: there was to be no permanent urban underclass. They were extraordinarily successful in moralising the urban poor without heavy-handed use of government, indeed, they saw this as part of the problem. Drunkenness, crime and illegitimacy all decreased during the second half of the nineteenth century – the high point of limited government and free trade.

Some conservatives reacted to the instability and dynamism of Victorian England by a retreat into nostalgia for a medieval past. Disraeli and the Young England movement of the 1840s hoped for a return to a sort of medieval community as an alternative to industrialism.

Nostalgia has a powerful and indeed legitimate political appeal. In a country with a history like ours, where the National Trust is the largest voluntary association, any politician is going to be tempted to mould his arguments in the form of an appeal to the past. We see it in today's political debates about social change. If some Conservatives look back to 'real families' of a man earning a family wage and his wife at home looking after their children, so the Labour Party looks back nostalgically to 'real jobs', when the man was working all his adult years on the production line of some heavy industry which has long since gone to the Third World. The irony is that those traditional jobs and those traditional families went together and neither can easily be sustained without the other.

Nowadays one might think that for the Labour Party the ideal is the 1940s and for the Conservatives it is the 1950s. Critics may attack Conservatives for looking back fondly to those potent images of life in the suburbs of the 1950s, but anyone following the work of left-wing intellectuals such as David Hare can see that for them the period to celebrate is what is thought to have been the intense national community of the wartime years and immediately afterwards.

There are still lessons to be learnt from the historical debates of the 1940s and 1950s. Richard Titmuss gave the classic socialist interpretation of the 1940s, arguing that 'the circumstances of the War created an unprecedented sense of social solidarity among the British people, which made them willing to accept a great increase of egalitarian policies and collective state intervention'. But there are two problems with this claim. First, wartime may create an intense feeling of national purpose, but it is no model for the life of a civil society in peacetime. To regard a society at war as any sort of model for peacetime is to take a dangerous step on the path to totalitarianism: the tragedy was that the Second World War confirmed in us our fatal trust in government as benign and rational. Second, there was a good deal more detachment, scepticism and cynical humour in the 1940s than is now allowed for. Ministry of Information surveys of popular attitudes at the time show that people were most concerned about their personal and family safety and about winning the war, rather than with issues of social justice or post-war reconstruction.

If we move on to look at the 1950s we can see the national mood was extraordinarily sensitive to fears about the damage done by free markets and remarkably relaxed about the damage done by big government. The pundits feared that commercial television was going to threaten our national culture. Looking back we can see that it was the destruction of the old communities by the enormous new public sector housing estates, a bipartisan policy trusting to big government, which did far more damage. Throughout the post-war period public debate in this country has been preoccupied with the damage to traditional British values supposedly threatened by brash market forces whilst at the same time the real threat was coming from the intrusive state. It is as if, like the guns of Singapore, we are armed against the wrong enemy, ready to repel an assault from the forces of vulgar American capitalism, whilst our society has really been under threat from the enormous powers of our own state.

When the historians finally reach a detached assessment of the 1980s the picture will look very different than today's conventional wisdom. At the moment we are told it was all about the triumph of market forces. The truth about the 1980s is that the serious policy mistakes were a result of the drift away from free markets. Especially after the 1987 general election, the government passed too much 'bad law' — laws which shared the common feature of giving ever more power to the state. Government was imposing new costs on the private sector, but instead of showing up as increased public expenditure, costs were imposed through heavy-handed regulation: they might not have appeared on the fiscal balance sheet but they were just as real to the private sector. The Financial Services Act, the Children Act, the Charities Act and the Food Safety Act all imposed heavy new burdens on the private sector without any rational calculation of costs and benefits. The idea of the state as enabler, purchaser or contractor, contains a great deal of sense, as I shall discuss later. But it must not be distorted by the pernicious belief that Whitehall knows best and thus become a ground for yet more heavy-handed intrusion in the affairs of civil society.

How did the 1980s compare with the 1970s? In the 1970s the government was spending a higher percentage of GDP and was intervening in the economy far more. Did this somehow enable us to achieve a moral consensus as a nation, a greater sense of community? Was there less materialism and greed? Far from it, instead we had a Hobbesian war of all against all, fought with the state as the battleground. Each interest group was trying to capture the state for its own purposes, whether it was to obtain subsidies or receive tax breaks. As a result we suffered from the twin and related evils of overloaded government and ungovernability. In trying to do too much, the government merely found itself caught between a multitude of inconsistent claims for 'social justice'. Rolling back the frontiers of the state was essential for restoring some degree of authority to government.

The conclusion to this brief historical excursion is a paradox. On the one hand Great Britain has a longer history and experience of free market transactions than any other society in the world. But equally we seem not to understand our own history and perpetually to fall prey to the belief that we need our government to intervene to protect us from these dark, hostile, outside forces. As a result we are always on the lookout for the threat from market forces and are remarkably slow to see the greater danger posed for our civil society from the encroachment of the state.

11: The Market and Beyond

The previous chapter tried to show that the free market is an integral part of our history. Conservatives who worry about the impact of the free market on our traditions need to recognise that the free market itself is at the heart of the British tradition. But not only does the free market suffer from misconceptions about its place in our history, it also suffers from misconceptions about its claims as economic theory. We need to get straight exactly what free market economics really claims and whether it is compatible with any recognition of values and institutions which stand outside the market.

The first crucial distinction to make is between the free market as an abstract model and as a real set of institutions and human actors. The free market is one of the most powerful analytical tools which the social sciences have developed; but market transactions only take place within a real set of institutions, a culture or tradition. Academic economists have by and large been uninterested in the cultural and institutional underpinnings of real markets (shown for example in their extraordinary naïveté about economic reform in the old Soviet bloc). It is free marketeers with an understanding of conservatism who are best placed to explore the connections between the market as it appears in economic theory and the market as a social reality. This makes it all the more surprising that Conservatives failed during the 1980s to show how we understood these essential underpinnings to the market. It is what distinguishes us from pure economic liberals who see us all simply as individual economic agents floating freely, untrammelled by ties, culture or history. It is the aim of this chapter to explore the links between the abstract model of economic transactions and the reality of the market as an institution. The aim is to show how market transactions may only happen within an institutional framework and that market transactions themselves can help to sustain non-market institutions and values.

Arnold Toynbee offered a vivid and repellent picture of the free market, a world inhabited by 'gold-seeking animals, stripped of every human affection, forever digging, weaving, spinning, watching with keen undeceived eyes each others' movements, passing incessantly and easily from place to place in search of gain, all alert, crafty, mobile'.[36] This is how many of today's critics of the free market see it. We are all supposed to be atomistic individuals, pursuing our own self-interest and incapable of recognising any ties to people and institutions which are more than economic. On this sort of model, the free market is at best an unpleasant necessity: it would deserve no place at the heart of conservatism.

This visceral British suspicion of the free market rests on serious misunderstandings of free market economics. For a start, free market economics is not an account of human motivation. It has no pretensions to be a psychological theory. Believers in free markets are no more committed to saying that everyone is motivated by personal greed than to saying every tennis player at Wimbledon is simply motivated to win by the prize money. The players may be driven by any emotion from pride to wishing to please their parents, but we can say that, by and large, the best tennis comes from matches in which the players compete to win within the framework of the rules.

Free market thinkers have gone beyond this, however, and shown how even without appealing to such attractive qualities as benevolence or altruism and simply using the highly schematic model of us as economic agents, it is still possible to offer an account of the emergence of co-operative institutions. This is because within a competitive environment, co-operative behaviour may be the most efficient. Institutions which have a non-market logic of their own may thrive within a market environment.

Let us go back to the tennis match, but this time it is a game of doubles. One couple are radical individualists; each goes for every shot, they shamelessly poach off each other and each is concerned much more about how he or she performs than about their performance as a unit. On the other side of the net is a much more co-operative couple, they respect their partner, give way to each other, understand that each of them is only one part of a greater unit – the team. The chances are that a ruthlessly competitive tennis match will reveal the weaknesses of the first couple and recognise the competitive strength of the co-operative pair.

This is clearly relevant to the experience of modern capitalism. A Western businessman once described to me how his factory had been visited by a delegation of industrialists from the old Soviet bloc. What had amazed them above all was that the workers on the shop floor were not directly and continuously supervised. In the East the only way to ensure that a factory worker worked hard was to have a foreman almost literally standing over him – a sort of industrial equivalent of the secret police. This was not only unpleasant, it was also an incredibly wasteful way of running an enterprise. It makes much more sense if employees are motivated, feel part of a larger team to which they are committed and want to do their best.

Modern management techniques are precisely about creating a sense of co-operation and teamwork within the enterprise, because it is those types of enterprises which enjoy enormous efficiency gains and are thus rewarded in the open competitive market place. This is where the Japanese example fits in. We are often told that Japan is a model of capitalism very different from that in the West: let us assume, for the sake of argument, that this is true. We are told that we need to learn from Japan that lifetime employment, a commitment to the long term, not to mention worship of the company god, are all much better than traditional Anglo-Saxon capitalism. But what is the evidence that it is better? The evidence is that Japan has been an enormous economic success. Many of its industries have outperformed our own. Japan's institutional arrangements are rewarded in a competitive market environment. Many firms in the West are now trying to learn from Japanese industrial practices and absorb them. This shows that modern capitalism does not necessarily destroy ties of affiliation and loyalty but may well reward them because they also happen to be efficient.

The market makes no moral judgement about these arrangements, even though we personally will want to. But it does force conservatives to focus on one of the big issues in economic and political theory – the point at which external, market-based contractual arrangements should cease and internalised arrangements based on co-operation or authority should take over. Modern economic theory of the firm focuses above all on defining the boundaries which determine where external market style transactions should be displaced by internalised transactions based on authority, co-operation or teamwork. The firm constitutes one boundary where the market stops. The firm itself is, in the language of economists, a sort of 'market failure'.

This choice between an internal model of co-operation and an externalised market model is not a choice between good and evil, altruism and selfishness. The market itself is, in a sense, a co-operative institution in that it enables people with diverse backgrounds, purposes and desires to serve each others' interests through free exchange. For the wheels of capitalism – the specialisation of labour and trade – to turn, it is necessary for economic agents to have different skills and tastes. It is the paradox of co-operation through the free market that the co-operation is often between people we may not know and whose tastes and values may be very different from our own – the people who have made my child's toy may be living on the other side of the world in a culture far removed from mine.

Capitalism integrates us into what is rapidly becoming a single global economy. It creates a sort of community of interest without creating a community of values or of sympathy. For the pessimist it will be depressing that it does not necessarily create a community of values amongst market participants. But for the optimist the achievement will be that, even when no shared values are to be found, there is nevertheless the possibility, through market transactions, of working together for mutual benefit.

The boundaries between this internal and externalised co-operation are permanently shifting in response to a range of cultural and technological influences. The biggest single influence is probably the method of handling information. Modern technology has made explicit pricing possible in areas where it was not possible before. Within a decade we will probably be paying directly for tap-water by the gallon, for each individual television programme we watch and for every half mile we drive on a crowded city road. This is not some evil aggrandisement by the market; it is just that the costs of collecting the information necessary to price these goods and services is falling so dramatically that it will be possible to bring them fully within the range of the market. But equally in some other areas of human life, the advance of technology has caused a retreat from market transactions. We now have equipment at home for cooking or cleaning instead of paid servants, which many households would have had a century ago. The cost of a washing machine is now so low relative to the cost of a washer-woman that by and large the labour market has withdrawn from these transactions. In Chapter 15 I shall explain how these arguments are relevant to the internal organisation and structure of the public sector.

So far, I have clarified three particular features of the market. First, it is not a theory of human motivation: market participants can have an enormous variety of purposes. Second, the market can itself reward co-operative behaviour as it may also be efficient. Third, the boundaries which divide internal institutional arrangements for ensuring that people serve each others' purposes and external market-style arrangements will permanently shift. It is wrong to regard such shifts as somehow a battle between good and evil.

There is a fourth point to add to this list – that the market will also create circumstances which favour co-operation in another way, by the very process of mobility itself. Mobility is perhaps the most significant aspect of a market and it is the most ambiguous in its effects. Let us start with the obvious appeal of mobility, which nobody now can resist – that it enables the individual to make his or her own way in the world, seizing the benefits of equality of opportunity which no one nowadays could possibly oppose. The market hates waste and the greatest waste of all is people who are not given the opportunity of realising their potential. The most powerful force for breaking down the barriers of discrimination by sex or race or background is the market itself which will not want talents to go to waste. These are the roots of a modern, mobile and meritocratic society.

The irony is however that it is precisely this liberating power of the market, so widely welcomed, which also helps to explain some of our worse discontents. Consider how the concept of the 'ghetto' has changed over the past fifty years. A traditional ghetto was an entire group suffering systematic discrimination, such as Jews in Europe or blacks in America. It developed its own sense of community, its own hierarchies and sense of order as everyone, regardless of their abilities, found themselves trapped in the same way. What happens to such a ghetto if the barriers start to come down and suddenly its inhabitants can move in every sense –

geographically, economically and socially? The people with drive, exceptional ability and self-confidence take their chance and move out. What is left behind is a ghetto transformed into something far worse than before – a group of people who find it hard to command a good income in an increasingly meritocratic society and who find themselves without community leaders and models of success to look up to and hold their community together. They lose out as the institutions which would give a shape to their communities and their lives are weakened. This is why the Harlem of the 1990s is a much worse place than the Harlem of the 1940s. And on a much less dramatic scale such forces have been at work in Britain as well. The clearest case is probably the Catholics of Northern Ireland where, as the barriers have come down, we at last see a successful, well-integrated Catholic middle class. The Catholic communities left behind suffer the same sort of social collapse as some of the black inner cities of America. The problems of social collapse in inner city areas and sink estates have been widespread across advanced Western economies since the Second World War. It is a testament to the shallowness of the British preoccupation with public spending and the state that so many people have analysed these problems solely in terms of public spending, social security benefits and public sector house building. The truth is that we can only understand these problems if we appreciate that they are linked to the mobility and openness of a modern free market economy – one of its most attractive features.

It would be wrong to stop the analysis there, because it is misleading to focus on the effects of moving away from communities without also looking at the strength of communities people move to. Most people have seized the chance to live in the kind of community they want to live in, with the sort of neighbours they want to have. This brings people together by choice rather than circumstance. It is a change from which many people in our country have derived great benefit.

The market order which I have been describing may not always be moral or beautiful - though it is usually elegant and efficient. But neither is it pernicious or evil. It is non-moral rather than immoral. It is the background against which individuals and institutions must pursue their own purposes. The Church, wrestling with the problem of the cost of maintaining surplus churches in areas where the church-going population is shrinking, or the academic wondering at what price to sell his book attacking Thatcherism, are confronting the laws of supply and demand in the same way as the businessman selling his widgets. If we accept it as the essential environment within which we all must pursue our purposes, then political debate will finally have escaped from a tedious and sterile opposition to the market.

12: Civic Conservatism

The free market is the cutting edge of modern conservatism. It is the free market above all which has yielded much of the intellectual creativity and the political dynamism of conservatism over the past two decades. But many of the uncertainties and confusions in conservatism at the moment come from a creeping recognition that the free market, like patriotism, is not enough.

Values ranging from particular virtues, like honesty and fairness, through to ties of affinity to the wider community, constrain the market. These values are sustained by non-market institutions which help to shape our behaviour. And the free market actually needs these values in order to operate: they provide the cultural and moral environment it needs. If that environment does not exist then the market itself cannot take root – a problem which is becoming obvious in the old Soviet bloc. If private enterprise has been criminal for seventy-five years it is very difficult to create a new understanding of the boundaries between commerce and crime. If money lacks any sense of legitimacy, commerce just seems a refined form of theft – and that is an unsatisfactory base on which to build a modern free market economy.

The pernicious error, upheld by so many of our *bien pensants* and pundits, is to regard the market as the threat to the rich life of a civil society and the state as somehow embodying or protecting those values. The historical evidence offered in Chapter 10 and the economic theory explained in Chapter 11 show what a fallacy this is. The tragedy of twentieth-century Britain has been the way in which the state has taken over and then drained the lifeblood from a series of institutions which stood between the individual and the government. In his fascinating book on the British Constitution, Ferdinand Mount subtly analyses what he calls the 'thinning' of our understanding of the British Constitution.[37] Instead of appreciating all the checks and balances of a civil society, we have moved over the past century simply to a belief in the over-arching power of a sovereign parliament. But that process has not just gone on in our constitutional theory: we have seen it in practice too as our network of civic institutions has thinned. Gradually we have lost sight of the virtues of those institutions which thicken our social structure and give it a richness which is lost if it is just individuals facing a Fabian, centralised welfare state. Britain has been, if you like, 'deconstructed'. We have seen great and proud institutions such as our voluntary hospitals nationalised and brought under state direction: it is no exaggeration to say that the fate of Bart's hospital was sealed when it was nationalised in 1948 and lost control of its own destiny, becoming the tool of health planners. Other institutions, like the ancient universities, have become so dependent on public funds that they have fallen prey to the disease of believing that the best way to embarrass politicians into giving more money is to say how terrible things are. The behaviour of too many public sector bodies and their associated pressure groups reminds one of those nature programmes showing fledglings in a nest with beaks permanently open to attract the harassed parent. And as resources are inevitably finite, the battle is really to attract attention away from their rival siblings – a stark truth ignored in polite society. Once an institution has descended to this level, it has come to resemble a dependent infant and should not be surprised if it loses authority and respect.

The starting point for any authentically conservative approach has to be that Britain is not a 'lumpy' enough country. The rationalist agenda for the public sector throughout most of this century has been to eliminate diversity, which was always seen as indefensible discrepancy. Reformers have seen themselves as energetic pastry cooks, wielding a rolling pin to smooth out the lumps in the dough. They have ended up producing a state which is smoother, more fine-ground, than any other in the advanced Western world. England does look like a remarkably uniform unitary state compared with other advanced Western countries. In America there is a genuinely federal system. On the Continent the effects of large public sectors are softened by a much greater degree of local discretion than we have here. Germany has different rates of payment for health insurance in different sickness funds. In France a significant element of the welfare system is under the control of the local commune, where the mayor has enormous discretion. In Italy the local tax base is much sturdier than the national tax system. England seems to be neither one thing nor the other; it is too big for central government to have any genuine knowledge of local conditions, but not big enough, not spaced out enough for genuine local diversity to come easily.

This process has not just undermined old institutions like Bart's and ancient universities. As we industrialised in the nineteenth century, a network of voluntary organisations was created by working-class self-help: friendly societies, mechanics institutes and local guilds. Macaulay summarised it very well:

> This is the age of societies. There is scarcely one
> Englishman in ten who has not belonged to some
> association for distributing books, or for prosecuting
> them; for sending invalids to the hospital, or beggars to
> the treadmill; for giving plate to the rich, or blankets to
> the poor.[38]

They have all been weakened, if not destroyed by the advance of the state. And the tragedy is even more poignant because people still do not understand what has happened. Dr David Green, who has studied this subject in great depth, cites a radio programme in which it was argued that it was a disgrace to a civilised society that the Royal National Institute for the Blind was providing services for blind people which should be done by the state. But the real sign of a civilised society is precisely that voluntary, charitable organisations can meet human needs without coercive taxation and the employment of public officials. The way in which public debate about any social problem focuses almost entirely on levels of public spending is depressing evidence of how public understanding of these issues has also 'thinned'. It is this shift in understanding which conservatives need to combat.

There is a paradox also about these civil institutions which may help to explain why they have lost out in public debate this century. We value qualities – honesty, prudence, generosity – which stretch way beyond our particular neighbourhood. Moreover we take pride in our identity as citizens of a nation state. And so the government seems to occupy a superior position in the scheme of things because it can support or enforce patterns of behaviour which are uniform and nationwide. But the truth is that local institutions exercising power and authority locally may be better able to sustain those values than nationwide institutions. A detailed and over-prescriptive national curriculum might be a less effective device for raising standards in education nationwide than giving local head teachers greater power in the running of their own schools, and parents the greatest possible power to choose between them.

The challenge facing both main political parties now is to formulate a coherent set of policies which shows that, as well as for the individual, there must be a role for collective action, but that collective action does not necessarily mean state action. The race is on. And as it is being run, the first thing to remember is that those institutions which stand between the individual and the state, giving life so much of its meaning, thrive in a free economy where they are not weakened by the burden of high taxes and the suffocating bear-hug of high spending. The biggest threat to collective action comes from the state.

Civic conservatism thus places the free market in the context of institutions and values which make up civil society. Conservatives believe in the free market but as a part of a civil society with limited government and free institutions. One name for this line of thought which may spring to mind is the social. The Ordo-Liberal exiles from Hitler's Germany who coined this term understood, as their name implies, that a market has to function as part of the social order. It can only function, for example, if prices carry out their essential job of conveying micro-economic information, hence the crucial role of the independent central bank. Strong and stable families are equally part of this social order, hence the ambitious Family Law in Germany explicitly setting out obligations between the generations in a family.

Nevertheless there are two difficulties with the term 'social market'. The first is the fatal ambiguity as to whether 'social' is being used as a qualifier or a describer. The Ordo-Liberals meant a genuinely free market which would thus, by definition, be able to fulfil its social purpose, rather than Hitler's corporatism serving the interests of the military-industrial complex. But in Britain, the 'social' in 'social market' has a rather different implication - that somehow the market is a bitter pill which has to be sweetened with large dollops of public expenditure and state intervention. This misunderstanding of the 'social' is evidence of the impoverished state of our political language.

The second difficulty with the concept is that it is difficult to detach it from its German origins. The reconstruction of Germany after the Second World War has been one of the triumphs of Western political design, rivalled only by the construction of the United States of America after their War of Independence. In both cases a new political order needed new political and philosophical foundations. The 'social market' was a concept which carried out this role for the Germans. But in Britain, because of the extraordinary continuity of our political and legal arrangements, the bonds which tie us together are much more historical and less conceptual. One of the problems which our rationalist reformers encounter is that they imagine that somehow we could all unite behind some explicit new constitutional settlement, without having to undergo the crisis of military defeat or rebellion from our sovereign power.

Oddly enough at the same time as the Germans were developing the idea of the social market economy the One Nation Group was formulating a set of ideas which constitute one of the high points of conservatism. The role of the One Nation Group has been widely misunderstood in the Conservative Party. It was not a bunch of what would now be called 'Wets', but instead a group of young conservative thinkers, such as Enoch Powell, Angus Maude and Iain Macleod, who were rebelling against Baldwinian corporatism, and the nearly Bennite socialism of Harold Macmillan's tract, misleadingly called *The Middle Way*. In 1950 they stated:

> To a Tory the nation is not primarily an economic entity. It may place political and social ends above purely economic ones, and for their sake may justifiably on occasions seek to prevent change or divert it. Yet economic change is the normal environment in which nations live, and successful adjustment to it is a condition of their well being. In six years of war and six of socialism this important truth was dangerously obscured

and overlaid. We doubt if it yet claims sufficient attention.[39]

This conservative insight, a commitment to the free market, sustained by a wider set of values which in turn enables institutions to thrive free of state control is at the heart of conservatism. It stands in clear contrast to two other positions – neo-liberalism and traditionalist communitarianism.

Conservatives have made a useful alliance of convenience with the free market neo-liberals and fought many of the battles of the 1980s with them. But a conservative realises that, in Quintin Hogg's neat expression, economic liberalism is 'very nearly true'. The trouble with the neo-liberals is that they simply think in terms of the individual economic agent without any understanding of the institutions, values and ties which are not just good in themselves but are anyway essential for any real free market to thrive. They suffer from what T. H. Green called 'inveterate irreverence'. Everything is equally open to challenge. No distinction is made between the trade union closed shop and the royal family, between the dangers of welfare dependency and the entitlement to the contributory pension. The real debate within the Conservative Party is precisely about reaching these discriminating judgements and identifying where market reform is needed and where not. In doing so Conservatives are addressing what Disraeli in *Coningsby* called the 'awkward question' of 'what will you conserve?'

One of the most significant intellectual events of recent years, which has passed largely unnoticed is the collapse of neo-liberalism as a significant intellectual force within this country. Its fountainhead, the Institute of Economic Affairs, is now producing works by ethical socialists in praise of the family and by anguished Catholic capitalists. It was extraordinary, for example, how the 1993 Conservative party conference was described as moving to the Right, when the real significance of the party conference was that it showed that leading figures on the Right of the party were recognising that there was more to conservatism than the free market – they were keen to talk about the values which helped sustain a free market economy.

The other alternative now experiencing something of a revival is a rampant communitarianism which is perpetually on its guard against the market, which it treats as a threat to everything conservatives hold dear. John Gray is its most distinguished and attractive exponent. If the peril of the neo-liberals is their undiscriminating scepticism, the equal and opposite peril of these communitarians is to 'utopianise the present'. Anything which exists now, provided it has a history of more than about five minutes, is praised in sub-Oakeshottian prose and absorbed into the precious web of British national identity. Any attempt to change it is to be denounced as cultural vandalism. This view fails to appreciate the cohesive and dynamic role of the market and instead tries to protect us from what it sees as the market's barbarity and harshness. The trouble is that it can lead to the dangerous temptation to opt out from the market environment within which individuals and indeed whole nations must inevitably make their way. Because by and large in British history our governments have been benign, not dragging us into evil wars, or in the words of Queen

Elizabeth I 'making windows into men's souls', the communitarian underestimates just how much damage big government can do. We are all aware now of the damage which modern industrial power can do to the environment; but perhaps we do not yet have a sufficient sensitivity to the damage which enormous concentrations of economic, political and legislative power in the hands of government can do to our moral and cultural environment. Even when we try to do good we may do harm. As has been observed, in the past we used to suffer from social evils, now we suffer from our remedies for them.

The conservatism of all the great British conservative thinkers, from David Hume and Adam Smith through to Enoch Powell and Michael Oakeshott is an attempt to avoid the twin perils of crude neo-liberalism and a retreat into the cosy embrace of big government as the only vehicle to protect our cultural identities. That commitment both to the free market and to some wider sense of community provides the creative tension which means that this conservatism, 'civic conservatism', yields more practical insights than either of its simpler alternatives. It is by its practical relevance that civic conservatism is best judged and it is to that which I now turn.

The theme of this investigation is the right institutional environment which a free market needs in order to thrive and which in turn can only thrive under a free market. The practical applications of such an approach are particularly relevant to three contemporary political topics – the conduct of economic policy, the future of Europe and our own anxieties about social change in Britain.

The transformation in the Treasury's approach to economic policy-making over the past decade has been dramatic. In the 1980s, when I served as an official in HM Treasury, the Treasury saw itself as holding a monopoly of economic policy-making. Because of the its responsibility for public expenditure control, the Treasury had become used to regarding every outside body as just another pressure group pleading its own cause and after either public money or legislative favours. Macro-economic policy-making was a matter of formulating the right financial rules and then sticking to them. Over the past few years the Treasury view has shifted dramatically. It is now understood that one of the best ways of assessing whether or not the economy is in an unsustainable boom, or whether it has the prospects for continuing low inflationary growth, is to judge the amount of spare capacity in the economy, the gap between what can and what it is actually being produced. That in turn requires close contact with industry and taking their views seriously. Setting aside the government's wider interest in improving our competitiveness, a dialogue with industry therefore helps the Treasury's ability to deliver the right financial policy.

In addition, the focus for the conduct of monetary policy has shifted from rules towards institutions. In the past Conservatives thought you earned credibility by publishing a rule and sticking to it. Now they understand that you can gain credibility not by setting up the Treasury as the sole arbiter of financial policy but by bringing a greater interplay of different opinions and institutions into the formulation of policy. This is the reasoning behind creating a panel of independent forecasters and it also lies behind the move towards giving the Bank of England a greater degree of practical independence. These changes could be summarised as a shift in economic policy away from achieving credibility through rules towards achieving credibility through institutional diversity.

Similar institutional issues come up in the debate about the future of Europe. Again, some theorists seem to be suffering from serious misapprehensions about what a free market Europe should look like. Some free marketeers, influenced more by the perfect competition of the text books than by the understanding of real competition from economists of the Austrian school, can only think of competition in terms of a level playing field. This is not just a ghastly cliché; it is positively misleading as an account of how a competitive market works. It is not necessary for free competition that employees in competing firms all have the same terms of employment, that their firms have identical legal obligations, let alone that the employees all drink tap water of the same purity. People with this sort of model of genuine competition soon end up concluding that we should ban imports from the Third World as that is 'unfair' competition. In reality, competition is precisely about competition between different ways of doing things, different economic and social arrangements.

The secret of Europe's dynamism over the past few centuries is specifically that it comprised a series of different nation states – no one authority could suppress scientific experiment or free thought across the whole of Europe. If your prince did not like what you were saying, you could always flee over the border to another country where you could practice your religion or carry out your research freely. This should equally be the source of Europe's economic vigour. It is not that Britain wants to be the sweatshop of Europe – hourly pay rates are by no means the heart of the economic argument – it is much more to do with the ability to employ labour flexibly and have the legal framework that we want. Again, a diverse Europe with genuine national differences is better than one where all differences have been rolled out by some manic groundsman pursuing that vision of a perfectly level playing field.

There is not space within the confines of this book to develop these arguments in the areas of economic or European policy. Instead, I will focus on social policy questions and how civic conservatism may contribute in practice to our understanding of these social issues as a given indicator of sensible ways of trying to address them.

13: What kind of people are we?

Our deepest fear about the direction our country is taking is that somehow we are becoming worse people – more self-centred, more aggressive, hostile to excellence and achievement, less civil and less willing to give time and effort to any cause greater than ourselves. We see faces in the street or at the wheel of a car with the coarse brutality of a soldier or a peasant in the background of a painting by Breughel.

How real is this change? Are we indeed experiencing what one book has entitled 'a loss of virtue'?[40] If there is a change, is it to be attributed to the free market? What if anything can government do about it? No questions are perhaps so important and none more difficult for a politician to address, as they have no special claims to moral superiority. But the issues are so important that even politicians must be allowed to comment on them.

The critics normally muddle two completely inconsistent arguments. First, they claim that terrible changes are indeed happening and the blame lies with the free market – a claim I have already reviewed. Then if ever a Conservative dare suggest that there is a problem, they are accused of whipping up a 'moral panic' and told that really there is not a problem at all. Yet clearly something is happening and we need to try to be clear what it is.

There are three large social changes that capture people's worries about the character of our lives – family change, long-term unemployment and increasing crime. I will look briefly at them in turn and then see how they come together in what some people call an 'underclass'.

Most of us spend most of our childhood in a household headed by a married couple. Most of us marry and have children. Most people still believe that it is best to get married when you want to have children. It is not that we have opted out of marriage, but rather that extra periods of rather different ways of living have been added to the life cycle. Instead of leaving the family home in order to get married, we leave the family home to live in lodgings or share a flat with other people our age. At the other end of the life cycle, given men die before women, there are a large number of widows living on their own, who do not appear in those statistics for households headed by a married couple. These extra stages to the life cycle mean that just a quarter of all households now consist of a married couple with dependent children as against 38 per cent of all households in 1961. The inference we are supposed to draw from this widely-quoted statistic is that we now encounter a rainbow of divergent lifestyles in place of the traditional family. But if we turn from measuring households to measuring people, we see that 75 per cent of the British population still live in a household headed by a married couple, a relatively modest decline from 82 per cent in 1961. The biggest changes have been longer transitions in and out of the family – above all a gap between leaving the parental home and establishing a new family home and then, much later, a longer period of widowhood.

More children are being brought up in families which break down or where their father has never been around. Of the 1.3 million lone parents in 1991 the largest single group, and the one increasing most rapidly, was of unmarried mothers, of whom there were 440,000 – approximately a third of the total – as against 170,000 in 1981 and 80,000 in 1971. Nobody, apart from the most constrained prisoner of political correctness, can seriously imagine that being a young, unmarried mother is a good option for either the mother or her child.

The most convincing explanation of the dramatic increase in the number of young, never married, single parents has been offered by the American sociologist, Professor William Julius Wilson.[41] He argues that the 'marriageable pool' is seriously depleted. Men who are good bets as husbands, 'marriageable' in his terminology, must be holding down a steady job with a good wage. But in the inner cities of America and Great Britain such men are increasingly hard to find. So if a woman wants children there is no one worth getting married to, to help bring them up. Another American social thinker, Charles Murray, has added a further element to this explanation.[42] He argues that, at the same time, benefits for single parents and priority access to public housing mean that the option of being a single mother has become easier to sustain. If there are not many reliable men, a woman can in effect marry the state instead.

One of the reasons for the decline in the pool of marriageable men is of course unemployment. Critics say it is all to do with the recession. One almost wishes the problem was that straightforward: then as the economy grows one could be confident the problem of young male unemployment would indeed disappear. But even at the height of the boom in the late 1980s there were still pockets of very high rates of male unemployment; and these are the areas where the young lone mothers are concentrated. The reasons for high male unemployment are far removed from the traditional account which focuses on the growth rate of the economy. It is much more to do with the problems of young men who themselves may come from unstable family backgrounds with poor educational achievements and who resent that the only wages they can command are so low. The factors affecting their performance are intangible, not just material. One of the most interesting analyses of the black youth unemployment crisis in inner city America found that the best predictor of whether or not a young black person would find a job, better than social background or educational achievement, was whether he or she went to church.[43] This is an interesting clue, to which I will return later.

The third social problem on my list is crime. We know a surprising amount about criminals. The most obvious fact staring us in the face is that crime is predominantly committed by young men. Professor David Farrington, Britain's leading criminologist, summarises what we know about these juvenile offenders as follows: they tend to be of low intelligence, hyper-active and impulsive; their parents have supervised them poorly with harsh and erratic discipline; their parents are disproportionately likely to be separated and their mother to have given birth as a teenager; they are likely to come from low income families living in over crowded conditions and their parents and siblings are themselves more likely to have a criminal record. Many young men will engage in a small amount of crime and a small number of young men will engage in a great deal of crime. The 1 per cent of males born in 1973 who were convicted of six or more offences by the age of seventeen accounted for 60 per cent of all convictions for that age group. The peak age of offending is eighteen years for men. This actually coincides with a peak of affluence for these young men because they are likely to be in unskilled manual jobs (although their long-term income prospects are not good, their disposable income may well be higher than their peers who are staying on at school or in higher education).

Most young criminals eventually give up crime and settle down. The strongest single reason given for abandoning crime is pressure from a girlfriend or wife. Even after adjusting for all other factors, married men are less likely to be engaged in crime. They also say they stop because penalties are tougher for older, more 'professional' criminals.

Connections are beginning to emerge between these changes in the structure of the family, unemployment and crime. Conservatives often become nervous whenever embarking on such observations. The fear which they have – and it is very understandable – is that identifying structural causes risks removing any individual's responsibility for his own actions. But just as a conservative free marketeer can believe in the laws of supply and demand and at the same time welcome the flair of individual entrepreneurs and businessmen, so conservatives can equally recognise that social and economic forces are at work, even though ultimately every individual's fate remains his or her own responsibility. Conservatives need to develop a much more confident respect for what the woman in the BT advertisement once called 'the ologies' because modern sociology and criminology support many distinctively conservative insights.

If we now return to these phenomena of family, unemployment and crime we can see some strong connections. Young men, aged fifteen to twenty-five are the crucial link. They are the ones who father illegitimate children and who women – often understandably – have no desire to marry. It is their long-term unemployment which causes the greatest instability, particularly in inner city areas, and they are responsible for the vast amount of crime. Whilst there are other social problems, such as the high divorce rate, or the tragedy of unemployed men in middle age or beyond who cannot get back into work, the fact is that the most serious social problems facing us can be traced back to these young males.

Whilst it is tempting to call them an 'underclass', we know that their values are not that different from ours. They are not rebelling against capitalism. They also want to settle down, have a good job and bring up a family. They are not highly motivated left-wing rebels. The classic student rebels of the 1960s and 1970s had, research now shows, particularly close relationships with their parents whom they respected. Today's young men in trouble are much more likely to come from broken homes and suffer from the absence of an authoritative father figure and the problem they face is that they cannot organise their lives or discipline themselves to get from their current circumstances to the sort of life they aspire to. One of their crucial problems is that they lack self-control, they are impulsive. If they see a girl, they grab her, without thinking of the consequences. If they see a hi-fi in a shop they smash the window and take it. If they are offered a job flipping hamburgers, or delivering pizzas they chuck it in after a short while because they cannot stick at it and do not see why they should accept the low pay.

Some pundits argue that the problem with these young men is that they have become shamelessly individualistic loners. They are the atomised individuals incapable of recognising any ties to anyone other than themselves, who appeared earlier in the vivid quotation from Arnold Toynbee (p.82). We have all heard criminologists and sociologists on radio and television saying that all these men are doing is putting into practice Mrs Thatcher's remark that 'there is no such thing as society'. But not only do these people fail to understand the real nature of the free market, they are also factually wrong in their account of how these young men behave. The men are sociable and gregarious. This is even apparent in the types of crimes they commit – juvenile crime is group crime. It is the older 'professional' burglar who is much more likely to be alone. And one of the reasons they cease offending is that they mature and stop going around in groups. These juvenile delinquents do have loyalties to causes greater than themselves. The trouble is that the deep human instincts to be social, which are as prevalent in a free market society as anywhere else, have been captured almost exclusively by their own peer groups. They hunt and fight in gangs, are influenced by their friends and will engage in extraordinarily risky behaviour in order to impress them. The trouble is not therefore that they are more self-centred, rather the problem is that their natural sociability and desire to be regarded by others is not being expressed either constructively or creatively.

It is tempting to say that we should be able to prevent this bad behaviour by identifying the trouble-makers at a very early age. We do know that an unstable or broken home increases the risk of someone getting into trouble in their teens and that the earlier someone starts offending the greater the risk. Any infant-school teacher worth his or her salt can pick out from their class of six-year-olds the ones who are likely to be in trouble in ten years time. Indeed one study found that a mother's ratings of her boy's difficult temperament at six months was a good prediction of problems later in childhood. The problem is the false positives. Research shows that teachers will correctly identify the youngsters who are likely to end up as criminals, but they will also identify others who are not. It is indeed the case that criminals are likely to come from broken homes, but it is a dangerous fallacy to reverse this and say that if you come from a broken home you are likely to be a criminal. It is very difficult to design programmes for groups that are at risk which do not label or assume the worst of children who do have their fates in their own hands and who are not going to make a mess of their lives.

The task facing public policy is therefore clear, albeit enormously difficult to deliver in practice. The challenge is to ensure that these young men make the transition from being children in the parental home to being stable parents themselves, without doing too much damage to themselves or the rest of society in the process. That process has become more difficult in modern societies as the transition itself has become more complex as young men spend longer and longer in higher education, training or unemployment before they finally settle down.

The challenge is to create a legal and institutional framework which helps these people come to adulthood. The public sector is failing them if it is largely devoted to helping them systematically avoid ever having to confront the consequences of their actions. It traps people into an infantile state where authority is never exercised, facts are never faced and self-destructive behaviour is tolerated until it is too late. Getting these sort of messages across to children by preaching at them is a pretty hopeless task, but it should be possible for them to experience these lessons through their own experience of institutions which are both benign and authoritative. This is where the practical experience of what works in helping young people come to adulthood ties in with the principles of civic conservatism set out in previous chapters. It is very difficult for the local institutions which really can help shape people's lives – schools, training schemes, the criminal justice system and children's homes – to exercise authority if they are systematically being turned into powerless recipients of instructions which come down from a central authority. I will now look at each of these cases in turn.

Schools are perhaps the most important public institutions of all. All the evidence suggests that even in the toughest areas a good school can transform people's lives and that in turn the crucial determination of the success of a school is the character of its head teacher. A head teacher needs to be a large figure (which does not necessarily mean authoritarian) who sets standards, inspires the children to live up to them and is aware of Ernest Bevin's crucial insight that 'the worst sort of poverty is poverty of aspirations'. Teachers working on the basis that their pupils are going to be systematically discriminated against and will find it very difficult to get jobs, will do much less than those who encourage the belief in their children that their future lies in their own hands. It is harder now to get away with discipline which is wayward and authoritarian, but a clear framework for behaviour at school, with open rules enforced by all teachers in the same way can make an enormous difference – so-called affirmative discipline programmes have a lot to offer here.

Parents have a remarkable ability to sniff out a good from a bad school. Unleashing parental choice is the most powerful vehicle of all for improving the quality of schools. Instead of looking to educational authorities and the Department for Education to tell them what to do, schools would instead look to parents and pupils and work out how they can best satisfy them. A fascinating case study of the power of this approach is Seymour Fleigel's book *Miracle in East Harlem* which describes how a radical liberalisation of the public school system in East Harlem succeeded in dramatically raising standards.[44]

One of the most substantial ways in which the state has expanded since 1979 is in higher education and training. Training is often recited as a sort of mantra which must inevitably do good, whereas in two ways it can actually do damage. First, it is no good if a central authority decides what training they think people need if it is not what employers themselves want. Training needs to be driven by individuals choosing what skills they want in order to improve the wage they can command. There is no point creating a system in which people being trained regard themselves as passive and empty vessels being filled whatever way the authorities think best. Second, there is some depressing evidence from America which suggests that training programmes for the unemployed can make things worse. In a classic American experiment one group of unemployed people were offered free training whilst the second group were not. A year later it was the unemployed group which had not been offered training who had experienced more success in finding jobs.[45] What is the explanation for this? It appears to be that training programmes do not just increase what economists call the 'human capital' of trainees, but they also increase their reserve wage, the sort of wages which they feel they ought to command after completing the training course. If the training course is oversold and ends up increasing the reserve wage by more than it increases their real earning capacity then it has created a yet greater obstacle in the way of their finding jobs.

Training schemes can help people in work boost their skills and hence their pay, but they are not always so effective at helping unemployed people find jobs. Indeed, the most effective programme of helping unemployed people back into work is not elaborate training schemes at all, but Job Clubs. They appear to be particularly successful in giving unemployed people the sense of purpose and control of their own lives which helps them into work. They are in many ways the secular equivalent of the evangelical churches whose effect on black unemployment was referred to earlier.

The criminal justice system too often operates like a classic bad parent – unpredictable, wayward, by turns lenient and harsh. Everything we know about juvenile delinquents indicates they are classic short termists with no sense of the long-term consequences of their actions. That means they need to experience a criminal justice system which responds rapidly, firmly and predictably to their misbehaviour. Instead too many so-called reforms have made the system ever more drawn out and incomprehensible. The process between being caught throwing the brick through the window or mugging the old lady and the final punishment is long, complicated and unpredictable. The police have to decide whether or not to let you off with a caution; the probation service has to investigate; the social workers have their say; the court hearing is delayed. By the time the young tearaway ends up in court it seems totally unconnected with the crime he may have committed six months earlier. And then the court hearing itself, which should be full of significance, can easily degenerate into tedious triviality. Seeing a teenager appear in court for the first time chastened and worried and then leave a quarter of an hour later with a cheeky smile of relief, as he discovers it does not mean anything after all, gives a depressing sense that one of our last chances of rescuing him has been lost. Too much of the debate about crime within the Conservative Party focuses on short, sharp punishment (useful though that may be) and not enough on the need for short, sharp handling of offenders, so that they rapidly confront the consequences of their actions.

In children's homes, the Children Act of 1989 has created doubt among many social workers as to exactly what physical powers they have to restrain children and exercise authority over them. One police officer assessed the situation very shrewdly. He observed that there was no point ever using excessive force but equally young tearaways in contact with authority had to know that ultimately the people in authority would win. If they knew that beyond a certain point social workers would be powerless to restrain them and had no powers to confine them to the children's home, then they reached the dangerous conclusion that authority could safely be ignored if not mocked.

The theme which connects these particular cases is always that the public sector in its contacts with young people needs to be able to exercise authority and guidance. That is not a matter of being wayward or dictatorial, but of the steady exertion of authority and the setting of a clear framework within which young men must live their lives. The local institutions with which young people are in contact need to be authoritative and powerful. But they cannot be like this if they are merely the outposts of an elaborate public sector bureaucracy. Setting them free from centralised control so that they are important local civic institutions is crucial to enable them to do the job of helping shape the lives of the young people with whom they are in contact.

14: Welfare and Behaviour

Three different schools of thought dominate the current British debate on the welfare state – the spenders, the cutters and the technocrats.

The spenders believe that the welfare state has enormous power to do good and if more money is spent more good can be done. But they never accept it can also do harm. If a social problem is identified, and it is feared welfare spending is making it worse, the welfare state suddenly becomes a puny and irrelevant thing which reacts to people's behaviour without apparently ever changing it: it reflects society without affecting it.

The cutters are not interested in the finer points of what the welfare state may or may not be capable. They talk as if it is like champagne: it might be marvellous, but the trouble is we simply cannot afford it. In Britain much of the debate about social policies focuses on the cost of the welfare state and relatively little on its social consequences. We are more comfortable talking about its impact on the public finances rather than on private behaviour.

The third school are the technocrats who have ingenious wheezes – a negative income tax, a social dividend, a new hypothecated tax – all of which seem to solve the taxing and spending dilemma by muddling it up so it is impossible to tell what is being paid in and what is being paid out. These elaborate schemes always seem to avoid addressing the crucial distributional question of who gains and who loses and why.

The problem with these approaches is that they do not

capture what most people think the welfare state does. It is first and foremost a mutual insurance scheme to which we all contribute when times are good and from which we all expect to draw when they are not so good. It works in this way because we are all at risk to some extent from the vagaries of ill health, unemployment and old age. The welfare state also operates as a device to transfer resources to people whose misfortunes we are unlikely to share but to whom we feel an obligation. Ultimately both of these functions – the mutual insurance function and something much more like traditional charity – rest on some sense of shared values. A mutual insurance scheme would not work if we felt that some people were deliberately running their lives in such a way as to put as little into the pot as possible while taking out as much as they could. As for the charitable function, this also rests on a belief that the people we want to help are the victims of misfortunes we can sympathise with and have not simply made different choices about how to live their lives.

The welfare state may help a modern economy run efficiently but ultimately we can only justify taking approximately a quarter of our entire national output through coercive taxation by some moral obligation to fellow members of our community. The classic view set out so eloquently by William Beveridge assumes that all citizens of this country are automatically members of this community. We have duties to our fellow citizens in Bristol and Birmingham that we do not have to people in Bologna or Bremen. (There are fewer more intensely nationalist institutions than the modern welfare state.) We would all like to think it was that simple. But the argument which is beginning to surface is what, if anything, does this shared citizenship entail: is any behaviour to be expected? Can any conditions be set other than simply being a citizen of this country?

We can already see evidence of this sort of deeper question in popular concern about foreigners claiming entitlement to British benefits, or benefits being paid to New Age Travellers. The sums of money involved may not be enormous, but the sense of affront to the community's values is intense. Most people belief that war widows should be receiving more in benefits than New Age Travellers – a crucial distinction which the technocrats, preoccupied with measuring income and its redistribution through means tests, completely fail to grasp. Most people believe that someone sacked as a result of the recession, desperately sending dozens of letters a week to possible employers is entitled to more help than someone not actively seeking work and engaged in petty crime to finance a drug habit. They expect these sorts of judgements to be reflected in the way in which the welfare state functions. If they are not and the welfare state becomes an entirely neutral device for transferring resources, regardless of behaviour, then the willingness to accept the high levels of coercive taxation necessary to finance it will gradually be eroded.

This bring us to the great dilemma facing the British welfare state today. On the one hand it helps to sustain and possibly even encourages a greater diversity of lifestyles. On the other hand we feel less of an obligation to finance ways of living which are profoundly different from our own. A large welfare state cannot encompas an increasingly diverse society.

The dilemma is vividly encapsulated by two extreme models for welfare states in the West – America and Sweden. America is the most diverse of the modern, liberal democracies. It has the greatest variety of lifestyles and the most modest nationwide welfare state. It would be difficult for example to persuade a Vermont farmer that he had obligation to help meet the housing costs of a Mexican immigrant in California through a federal system of redistributive taxation. Sweden is a small, homogenous, intensely conformist society and has the largest welfare state of any Western country. The dilemma which faces any politician, on the Left or the Right, is in which direction the British welfare state can and should be moving. It is naïve to imagine that somehow we can be as diverse as the United States, whilst at the same time operating a welfare state on the scale of modern Sweden. This seems to be the delusion to which the liberal advocates of the welfare state have fallen prey. It is the tension which lies behind much British confusion about the role of the welfare state. It is a challenge to those advocates of a system which is neutral about behaviour, unconditional and undemanding. This will end up with a 'lowest common denominator' system much more limited than today's, which still rests on Beveridgean foundations.

We are being forced to confront a problem which some like to pretend does not exist; but which was well understood by the founders of the welfare state. Beveridge did indeed have a universalist vision in which every British citizen would participate in his scheme; but he in turn assumed that people's patterns of behaviour were and would remain intensely conservative. Where he saw a risk of what would now be called 'moral hazard', such as unemployed people who were not actively seeking work, he was happy to lay down quite stringent conditions for receipt of benefit. Above all, the national insurance system on which the health service and the social security system were to rest was intended to capture the reciprocity of the welfare state. It was always intended to be a mutual insurance system into which we all paid when times were good and took out when they were bad.

Winston Churchill famously advocated national insurance when he served in Asquith's government on the grounds that 'I do not like mixing up moralities and mathematics'. He preferred an automatic system of national insurance contributions to discretionary payments from local poor law authorities. But what that famous quotation fails to recognise is that the very existence of an explicit contributory system is in itself a type of moral arrangement. It is a social contract available to all the citizens of this country.

Sadly we have seen a steady erosion of the significance of contributory benefits. It was envisaged they would be fundamentally different from the means-tested assistance available to those who had not paid their contributions. Instead the combination of pressure from the Left to raise the entitlements of non-contributors, and from the Right to save money, particularly by cutting back on the earnings-related element in contributory benefits, has combined to remove any sense that serious conditions have to be met before one can receive benefits.

We need to be more rigorous, then, in setting the conditions which are a prerequisite for full participation in the welfare state. Perhaps the most extraordinary feature of the British welfare state is how undemanding it is compared with Continental Christian and Social Democracy. We could afford to be undemanding in the past because we assumed we were such a cohesive national unit that nothing needed to be explicit. We could all assume we shared the same values. This is changing.

If we look, for example, at social security benefit rates, it is clear that we do indeed spend a much higher proportion of GDP on benefits than many other advanced Western countries, though it is also true, as the critics protest, that the levels of benefits are not particularly high. This shows that benefits go to far more people in Great Britain because the conditions for receiving them are much more relaxed. This was the logic underlying Peter Lilley's agenda for reform of social security and its significance and coherence were not fully appreciated. The best way both of saving money in social security and linking the system more closely to our assumptions about behaviour is to ensure that proper conditions for the receipt of benefits are set and then enforced. The unemployed need to be actively seeking jobs. Invalidity benefits should only go to the genuinely disabled. Help with housing costs should be conditional on those costs being reasonable.

At the moment, one criterion for receiving Income Support is simply being a single parent. Many mothers now work when their children are at school and there is a case for asking that single parents claiming Income Support should be actively seeking work when their children are of school age. With Family Credit boosting their incomes in work and Child Support payments staying with them as they get work, this would add up to a powerful agenda for getting single parents back in contact with the labour market.

We can learn from the continental welfare states how it is possible to set clear conditions for the receipt of some benefits. In France parents will lose their family allowance if their child plays truant from school. In Belgium you can lose benefits if both parents are not registered on the birth certificate. The use of the welfare state as a powerful instrument to reinforce some of the elementary rules of behaviour is to give it an explicitly civic function. If it is recognised that the welfare state is a powerful civic institution then we are entitled to try and use it to reinforce the shared values of the community. This same thought can also be put in much more market language: the welfare state rests on a series of contracts between us in our roles as receivers and taxpayers and it is worthwhile making these contracts more explicit than in the past.

Unfortunately some of the rhetoric surrounding some specific Citizens Charters has tended to exacerbate this problem. The language of citizens' rights and of consumer power is attractive provided it does not exclude any sense that the users of public services have to behave responsibly. It is not right to call a GP in the middle of the night over a trivial matter; you cannot expect a place at a college of higher or further education unless you have got the right qualifications; the police cannot be expected to solve every dispute with the neighbours. Many people working in the public sector may like to think that their all problems can be resolved by more public money, but often the problem is that they are finding themselves less and less able to exercise authority and more and more under pressure from users of their services, who are impatient and demanding. The private provider has the right to refuse to serve the unreasonable customer – from the pub which wants its customers to wear jackets through to the private school which expels the badly behaved child. If the public sector is to learn from the high standards of the private sector, as it must, then it is entitled also to set some conditions for receiving its services.

A second policy application which follows from this analysis is that we should also try to give greater local discretion for the provision of money and services through the welfare state. Whilst many people pay lip service to the ideas of great diversity and discretion, the widespread resistance to the social fund is a salutary warning of how in practice many people still want a uniform, over-regulated welfare state system. The social fund was a tiny attempt to bring a modest amount of local discretion into the social security system. It dispenses approximately £350 million out of the total budget now of over £80,000 million, yet it is still denounced as some fundamental attack on the British constitution because social security regulations no longer specify exactly when someone on Income Support is entitled to a payment for blankets for a cot or a set of gardening equipment.

Conservatives encountered similar difficulties when attempting to have Access Funds for poorer students administered locally by universities and college. What is a sensible shift from rule-bound benefits to genuine local discretion was resented as somehow improper. Again, whatever the platitudes we hear about diversity and local discretion we are still far from accepting them in practice. Anyone looking at this debate from the Continent would be amazed at the British preoccupation with nationwide regulation and uniformity. The local mayor and commune in France and the local authority in Italy have much greater power to dispense money in accordance with their judgements of need. This makes it much more possible to distinguish between deserving and undeserving cases in a way which a rule-bound system finds very difficult. We could perhaps go further in bringing discretion into the allocation of benefits by inviting charities to manage social fund payments locally.

Two further policy conclusions follow from a belief in this sort of welfare state which emphasises reciprocal obligations and is concerned with creating greater local diversity and discretion. These negative conclusions stand against some of the current fads of the group identified as technocrats at the beginning of this chapter. One of the fallacies which the technocrats commit is to assume that the only thing which the welfare state needs to take account of is income, and that our current social security system is a sad departure from the ideal of one over-arching means-tested benefit. But we may perfectly legitimately want to identify certain categories of people for whom we wish to pay more than others. We may want to say that a war widow should receive more than an unemployed single man. We may be willing to see students taken out of social security on the grounds that this is the wrong way of starting their adult careers – whereas the same argument does not apply for, say, pensioners. These are not judgements about the moral worth of individuals, but judgements about the relevant differences between circumstances of different groups. There is a logic to focusing on categories of claimants rather than entirely on the incomes of individuals.

A further policy conclusion also stands out against the current trend towards maximising the efficiency of the distribution of benefits by trying to carry it out with the minimum of direct staff intervention. No cause is more popular nowadays than cutting civil service numbers, but we need to recognise that sometimes this will make it more difficult to pursue other policy objectives. One example is the early Rayner scrutiny which recommended that manpower in Unemployment Benefit offices could be saved by not requiring unemployed people to sign on so frequently. Now many of the unemployed only have to sign on once a fortnight and for some it is even less often than that. Not only is this an open invitation to fraud, it also risks disconnecting the unemployed person from the labour market if there is no reason for getting out of bed in the morning and taking the bus into town. The truly efficient policy would be the one which had the unemployed signing on much more frequently.

The central message of this chapter is that the welfare state is about more than redistributing income and access to services. We also have to accept, whether we like it or not, that the welfare state must inevitably have an impact on people's behaviour and that we have to think about what those impacts might be. In many ways this is simply bringing us back to the old problem of moral hazard – that the greater the assistance offered to people in a certain set of circumstances, the more people will be in those circumstances in future. It opens up the real debate on the welfare state between those are only concerned with the here and now, the visible and vivid circumstances of someone in trouble, and those who look forward to the effects of such assistance on people's behaviour in the future. The dangerous short-termists are those who blithely set about expanding the welfare state without reflecting on its long-term implications for behaviour.

15: Reinventing Platoons

Fred Zimmerman's *High Noon* is one of the classic Westerns. Gary Cooper plays the sheriff who stays at his post knowing that three desperadoes, who he had captured years before, were coming to get their revenge after their release from jail. He goes round the town trying to find someone who will stand beside him, but no one is willing to serve as a marshal. The film was made in the 1950s and was taken as a critique of the alienation and selfishness in America's suburbia. It is a striking contrast with a more recent film, *Witness*, in which Harrison Ford takes refuge with the Amish community as he flees from corrupt policemen. One of the most moving scenes in the film is when the Amish come together to work for a day building a barn for a friend. At the end of the film when the bell is tolled to signify danger they all rush across the hills from their farms to assist the family and defeat the armed attackers. It is a vivid picture of mutual assistance in a particularly intense community. The two films portray the two extremes of the spectrum of community engagement.

Many people in Britain, from all political persuasions, might like to see us edge a little bit towards *Witness* and a little bit further from the narrowness of vision of *High Noon*. The practical, political question is which policies are most likely to yield these values. It is my opinion that a commitment to the free market, limited government and strong institutions, is by far the best suited for this purpose.

The practical test is what governments can do to strengthen the civil institutions of society. Perhaps the first thing is not to get in the way. The significance of the government's deregulation initiative extends far beyond economic burdens on business. It was a significant attempt to shift government out of what Douglas Hurd, in a different context, has called 'the nooks and crannies' of our national life.[46] It is deeply depressing to visit the local Meals on Wheels service and to be told they have had to cut back on the range of food for elderly people because of the Food Safety Act; to hear from the local children's playgroup how they have had to push up their prices beyond the reach of poorer mothers because of all the extra costs arising from the Children's Act or to hear from the charity trying to help poor people that none of its clients can now serve as trustees because of the financial risks which the Charities Act now imposes on them. The pernicious effect of heavy-handed regulation on local voluntary groups is greater than ever. Deregulation is therefore a crucial part of civic conservatism.

The government must also resist the temptation to be a monopolist. It must allow self-help to stand alongside tax-financed activity. One area where this is particularly topical is law and order. The police have always been wary of Neighbourhood Watch schemes developing into alternatives to them; but the reality is that the police are so hard-pressed now we can only expect Neighbourhood Watch schemes to take on some of the traditional functions of the bobby on the beat. It makes sense for 500 members of local schemes to club together and put in £20 a year each so they can employ someone to walk the streets of their neighbourhood at night keeping an eye on their houses and reporting anything suspicious to the police. It is no different from the occupants of a mansion block employing a security guard to stand at the entrance.

The public sector now includes so many important institutions that enhancing their power is an important part of civic conservatism. A variety of devices for achieving this have been developed over the past few years. We are all now learning to distinguish between purchasers and providers, linked in new contractual arrangements through competitive tendering, market testing and internal markets. At the same time a new status has been gained by, for example grant-maintained schools and self-governing hospitals. The market – contracts, choice, competition – is being introduced within the public sector so as to achieve the authentically Tory objective of strengthening local institutions. These institutions, once cowed by the centralising logic of a planner, can now gain a new independence, holding one side of a contract.

There are two different objections to this line of argument. First, the free market purists will say there is no such thing as a strong local public sector institution. They believe that if you want the good features of choice, competition and the market you have to shift to direct private payment for the goods and services now provided by the welfare state. Wherever it is sensible to move to full scale privatisation and private payment, we should do so. However the reality is that there are going to be services which remain publicly financed. This is not just a matter of political prudence, but also of political principle and economic efficiency. A minimal state is not necessarily the most efficient. It is a counsel of despair then to give up and say there is nothing that can be done to bring any of the good features of markets into publicly financed services. There are real decisions to be made about how publicly financed health care is delivered, what degree of autonomy is enjoyed by our publicly financed schools and how much diversity is to be allowed between different local authorities. Indeed increasingly we can expect to see political arguments between the Right and the Left focusing not so much on the boundaries of the state, but also on the nature of the state – how it discharges those functions which most people accept fall irreducibly to the public sector. The challenge is for the Conservative Party to show that it has a radical free market agenda which can be applied within the public sector which also serves the long-term Tory objective of strengthening the little platoons within society.

The second very different line of criticism of radical reforms within the public sector, for a long time came only from the most blinkered public sector unions and could easily be dismissed. Now there is a much more subtle and authentically Tory concern voiced by those critics, such as John Gray, who fear that a restless market ideology has replaced a genuine conservative regard for the traditional institutions of the public sector. They say that the health service, the education service and the armed forces rest on a series of subtle understandings which cannot be caught in the crude structure of a quasi-market contract. They argue the government is undermining the ethos of professions such as medicine or teaching. Hospital consultants, tea ladies in a naval base, scientific researchers in a university or Inland Revenue typists all feel as if they are the victims of a remorseless attempt to force everything they do into the straightjacket of a contract. It adds up to a significant challenge.

The first reply is simply that the changes going on in the public sector now are no more than the changes which the commercial world has been going through for the past ten years. The modern management consensus is that large organisations should stop trying to micro-manage from the centre. They should cut back on head office costs and give greater freedom to local managers to run their own show within a clear financial target. The changes in the public sector need not be seen as driven by political ideology but merely as catching up with changes other large organisations have already undergone. In my constituency of Havant there is a large IBM factory which has recently been given much greater freedom from head-office control than it ever enjoyed in the past. It can sell its products to other manufacturers, use alternative brand names and generate its own revenues. The speed at which the IBM factory in Havant has been given commercial freedom is much greater than the comparable process for the local self-governing hospital trust or the grant-maintained school. The pressure for change in IBM was driven by the rapid deterioration of its commercial fortunes. In the public sector, it is the constraints on public spending which should drive new thinking about better ways of delivering services. There is no more deadly threat to any serious reflection on how to improve the performance of the public sector than the simple minded belief that if only it were not for 'the cuts', which are only the normal constraints over public spending, then everything would be fine. In practice it is precisely the discipline of, for example, the freeze on running costs which will drive reforms which would otherwise not have been contemplated. Public sector pressure groups always asking for more money can learn from the scientist Rutherford, who observed as his team was trying to split the atom: 'We have no more money, now we must think!'

Critics see these changes as vandalism, destroying long established British institutions. But this is just another example of the British disease described in Chapter 10 – our extraordinary capacity to become nostalgic about really quite recent institutions. The precious institutions critics are trying to protect are sprawling empires only built up during the 1960s and 1970s. The sudden sentimental regard for them is on a par with the bizarre attempts at listing 1960s tower blocks. Before reform the NHS was an elaborate monument to central planning, largely designed by management consultants, such as McKinseys, for Keith Joseph in the early 1970s. Teaching hospitals enjoyed freedoms very much like those now available for self-governing trusts until they were brought within the management structure of the NHS in 1974. Similarly grant-maintained schools enjoy rather less freedom than used to be enjoyed by direct grant grammar schools, which again were only absorbed within the system, or obliged to become private, in the mid 1970s. These highly centralised systems, based on an absolute belief in national uniformity, are very recent creations. They cannot be regarded as the historical deposits of generations of practical wisdom.

This in turn raises the crucial question of how Conservatives define the institution which they are trying to preserve. The institution which people can understand and care about because they use it and see it is not the NHS, but their local hospital or GP practice. It is not some great entity called the education service, it is their school or university. Those critics who argue that our public institutions are under threat are approaching the question too abstractly. It is the local institution which matters and which should be strengthened by the internal market agenda. The real problem is that this agenda has not been pushed far enough. Contractual relations should liberate the producer, but the trouble is that too often the contracts now being negotiated in the public sector are absurdly detailed. Instead of specifying what the outputs are, they specify in enormous detail exactly how the job should be done. The explanation appears to be that each side of the contract feels trapped by the other. Purchasers, because they feel so insecure in their relationship with the providers of services, believe the only way to guarantee quality is to write in enormous detail exactly how the job should be done. If the producers of services genuinely felt that they had a variety of purchasers and if the purchaser knew that he could always buy from somewhere else this would give greater reality and credibility to the contact, which in turn would mean it did not have to be so over-precise.

The problem is that too many of these relationships are still seen as essentially managerial rather than market-based. The only managers which the health service or the education service need are within individual hospitals, schools and universities. The crucial skill now needed on the purchasing side is good buying and that involves being rigorous about quality but not trying to manage the entities on the other side of the contract.

Conservatives need to give the maximum possible freedom to the providers contracting with the public purchasers. The private finance initiative offers local providers enormous scope to cut their dependence on Whitehall for the allocation of capital and develop instead their own projects, privately financed. It should not become the exception but the norm. It is essential for strengthening local institutions' powers in dealing with the Treasury that they look outwards for private capital rather than up to Whitehall.

This contributes to a wider transformation of the public sector as it buys in more services rather than taking on the task of delivering them directly through publicly owned capital and public employees. For example, the public sector should never buy another computer – instead it should be purchasing computer services from outside organisations which take over the responsibility for owning and managing the equipment, updating and employing staff. This is how Ross Perot began in America and Britain needs its own Ross Perots. It is the opponents of this trend who are the blinkered ideologues who believe that the public sector is all about owning buildings and employing people, rather than about delivering services.

Where employees remain within the public sector they should be employed on flexible terms and direct by local institutions, rather than on some uniform nationwide basis. They need to break free of the old public sector pay rules – a freedom which many providers have been slow to enjoy.

This should in turn make it possible for them to pay more to experienced staff so that people can build up a career in one institution without having to move away or become a supervisor – one of the perennial problems which has weakened our public sector. These changes tie in with the wider civic conservative agenda. One sociologist has distinguished between two groups of professionals in any local community – the spiralists, who were moving through on their way up to their next posting, and the burgesses, who were genuinely putting down local roots and building up real local knowledge. The management of the public sector has left us with too many spiralists and not enough burgesses: thus weakening the local community. Stronger local institutions can help change this.

As well as being able to look out for private capital finance, local institutions should also be able to sell their services locally. This is not a matter of the Treasury suddenly slapping on charges for essential services that everyone uses, but instead a liberalisation so that people buy extras which are not currently available to them. There is a misconceived aversion within the public sector to providing any sort of service unless it is free and tax-financed. For example, many schools have been slow to open up after hours, providing supervision or quiet time for their pupils, although it would be of great help to working mothers, because they do not like the idea of charging for it, even though this would boost the school's revenues and would of course contribute towards paying for their supervisors. Similarly, GPs should be free to sell extras to patients on their lists – a sports injury clinic on a Saturday for example – which are never going to be priority users of public money. We need a private finance initiative for current spending as well as for capital spending.

Before we get carried away with this agenda for local discretion and diversity we need to address some big constitutional and economic questions. We saw one example of these difficulties in the 1993–94 report from the Public Accounts Committee denouncing the changes which the government has pushed through over recent years. It was a poor report, partisan in spirit and muddled in argument – not what one would normally expect from the PAC.[47] Nevertheless it struck a chord. We do need a new constitutional settlement for the public sector so that we are clearer about the powers and responsibilities of central government and those which really lie with local institutions.

For a start, people have to be able to make real choices and that means genuine variations in services. While we pay lip service to diversity, we are really very uncomfortable with the idea that any aspect of the public service should be different in Bristol, Birmingham or Bootle. We find ourselves trapped in an argument which holds that diversity must mean inequity, which has to be corrected by redistribution, which in turn means centralisation.

There is no problem with businessmen sitting on the boards of trusts or grant-maintained schools being free from the control of local education authorities, provided that patients and parents have a genuine choice between them. We then have to accept the consequences of those choices, even if they are not choices we ourselves would have made. When the case of the Hackney headmistress who had refused to allow her children to see *Romeo and Juliet* because of its 'blatant heterosexism' hit the headlines, many of us instinctively thought the headmistress must be doing a bad job. But it was refreshing to hear parents of children at the school saying their children had been taught better and had caught up with their reading since new headmistress had arrived. If they backed her and believed in what she was doing there was no case for the local education authority or anyone else to intervene.

We also have to allow providers to make mistakes and not require ministers to be held accountable for every one of them. I remember one conversation on this subject with a permanent secretary who said that there was an important paper to be written entitled 'The role of the PAC in the centralisation of British government'. The fact is that if we wish to encourage enterprise and initiative we cannot also expect the sort of traditional patterns of detailed accountability which we are used to in the public sector. Instead managers of these institutions must be under a different set of pressures — pressures from users of their services who are free to go elsewhere or from purchasers free to place their contracts elsewhere. We must not end up in a limbo where we have both lost more traditional forms of political accountability and at the same time failed to gain the more vivid types of quasi-market pressure.

Equally the Treasury needs to be willing to loosen its direct controls. The trouble is that old-fashioned Fabian centralisation is a good way of delivering public expenditure control in the short term, even though in the long term it builds up pressures for ever greater public spending and certainly undermines the efficiency of individual institutions.

One of the imaginative items in the 1992 Conservative election manifesto was the so-called 'popular schools initiative', enabling the schools which parents were choosing to expand rapidly. But this fell victim to the pernicious Treasury doctrine of the surplus place, and so a popular school cannot spend any money expanding its capacity whilst there were still schools with surplus places in the area. This has obstructed the genuine operation of the educational market. In the commercial sector it would be nonsense for a firm that came up with a better mousetrap to be told that it could not sell any more on the market because there was a surplus of mousetraps being produced by a less successful manufacturer. The Treasury argument of course is that a lot of public money is tied up in these surplus places, but it is worth investigating this claim more closely. There is obviously some capital tied up in under-used school rooms, but by and large this has now been written off and is of little value. The main cost is teaching staff who are not efficiently deployed, but this is an argument for a more efficient and more mobile teaching profession rather than penalising successful schools.

This is certainly a free market agenda, but equally it is a Tory agenda for giving back real power to local institutions. The ultimate value of these institutions is because of the knowledge which they accumulate that cannot be written down in contracts or captured by a central planner in Whitehall. They have tacit knowledge about how to do things and must be given the freedom to put that into practice.

16: Summary

In his fascinating paper 'The Idea of "Character" in Victorian Political Thought', Stephan Collini quotes one socialist commentator observing a century ago that:

> today the key word ... in economics is 'character' ... [the reason] why individualist economists fear socialism is that they believe it will deteriorate character, and the reason why socialist economists seek socialism is their belief that under individualism character is deteriorating.[48]

During most of this century the debate between free marketeers and socialists took a very different turn: it became an argument about which set of economic arrangements would best deliver growth and prosperity. That argument has now at last been comprehensively won by the free marketeers. But precisely at their moment of triumph they find that the argument is not over after all but is instead reverting to the form it took in the Victorian period – the last time free market economics was as intellectually dominant.

We are just beginning to open up these sorts of questions: it is an uncomfortable and difficult business. The critics fall into two camps. First, there are those who can be called the 'clever despisers'. They are an odd mixture of *bien pensants*, some socialists and neo-liberals who do not think there is a problem at all. But they are a declining group. Many feminists are now ambivalent about the permissiveness of the 1960s, wondering if it did not do rather less for women than they had hoped and rather more to liberate predatory male sexuality. Neo-liberals are beginning to recognise that the idea of the economic agent makes little sense unless that agent is embodied in a culture with a set of values – a lesson which is being vividly demonstrated in the fraught attempt at free market reform in the old Soviet Union.

The second group of critics are the pessimists who fear that we are impaled on a dilemma in which the free market that brings us the prosperity we all seek also undermines what Tocqueville called the 'habits of the heart' which make life worthwhile. John Gray, the most distinguished member of this group is fond of citing Wittgenstein's remark that 'trying to repair a broken tradition is like a man trying to mend a broken spider's web with his bare hands'. For this group things are getting worse and there is not much we can do about it.

In this book, I am attempting to see if there is a path forward which avoids the twin perils of dismissing the problem or giving way to a deep melancholy about our fate. In my book, *Modern Conservatism*, I tried to address these issues and show how the free market and the community are both deeply rooted in the Conservative tradition and are reconciled within it.[49]

Since then, the politics of 'community' has burgeoned and there is a danger that this seductive term will become meaningless through over-use. The crucial Tory insight is that a community has to be embodied in real institutions which are essential to sustain traditions, values and patterns of behaviour.

The weakening of our civic institutions as government

has encroached on them since the Second World War is responsible for much of our social discontents. The political debate then turns on the conditions in which a rich network of such institutions can flourish. My argument in this book is that strong institutions thrive in a free market with limited government. It is this commitment to strong self-governing institutions in a free market economy which constitutes civic conservatism.

A concern with the strength of Britain's institutions – both national and local – is at the heart of the Tory tradition. Addressing that concern is essential in representing the values of the quiet majority of the British people.

Part III:
Conclusion
by John Gray

For the Conservative Party there is a clear lesson to be learnt from the cataclysmic defeat that it suffered on May 1st 1997. In a post-ideological age elections cannot be won by parties that are divided on issues of doctrine. They can only be lost. But that central lesson is one that contains no comfort for Tories. What it teaches is that conservatism has no future. This is not because of the party's ageing membership, its exiguous finances or any of the other disabilities illuminated by the election. It comes from the absence of a credible Tory project. The Conservative Party is the site of a contest between two obsolete world views. Its damaging conflicts over Europe were symptoms of a deeper division between 'One Nation' Tories and Thatcherite free marketeers. Neither faction has begun to understand the changes that have transformed British society and the global economy over the past decade.

With Labour immovably encamped on the centre ground there is no place for the Conservative Party. Labour has absorbed all the enduring truths that were once preserved in conservative philosophy. It has accepted the essentials of the reforms of the Thatcher era. It does not contest the legitimacy of liberal capitalism. Labour's new agenda asks how the imperatives of a deregulated market economy can be reconciled with the needs of social cohesion. On this, the central dilemma of the age, the Conservative Party has nothing to say. As Winston Churchill said of an unappetising dessert, conservatism today is a pudding without a theme.

Conservatism has been undone. In part it is a casualty of global economic and cultural changes over which no government has much leverage. The late modern world is unkind to ideologies. The plural, hybrid, fragmented cultures of late twentieth-century societies have corroded and destroyed the stable allegiances that sustain socialism –and conservatism. Tories who celebrated the defeat of socialism in the triumphalist 1980s were not mistaken; but they failed to note that the forces that had rendered socialism obsolete were bound to do the same to political parties that had defined themselves by resistance to it. When socialism was removed from the agenda of history so was conservatism.

In part conservatism has been undone by Labour's uncompromising programme of modernisation. The lessons that Labour learnt from four election defeats were deep and hard. Central among them was the folly of framing policy or strategy in ideological terms. In modernising itself Labour only mirrored changes that had already occurred in the world. By doing so, however, it reinvented itself as a new party. For the first time since the age of Lloyd George the Tories found themselves in competition with a British centre party. It was a contest whose outcome was foreordained. A Tory party whose instincts and rhetoric had been forged in a conflict with social democratic corporatism was defenceless against a post-social-democratic party of the centre.

Conservatism was undone finally by the unintended – and, so far, still uncomprehended – consequences of Conservative policies. May 1st 1997 was a catastrophe in which the world's oldest and most successful political party received a lower share of the national vote than at any time since the beginning of British democracy in the Great Reform Act of 1832. In this spectacular débâcle the capture of the Tory Party by a callow New Right ideology played a crucial part. In Part 1, I wrote:

> In an irony that will delight historians in years to come, the political effect of the ephemeral intellectual hegemony of the New Right, in Britain and similar countries, has probably been to accomplish the political destruction of conservatism: it may have rendered conservative parties unelectable, perhaps for a generation.(p.5)

In one respect that judgement now needs amendment. There is little reason to think the Tories will ever recover. On the contrary, there are several rather strong reasons for thinking that the voters of England may follow those of Scotland and Wales and consign the Conservative Party permanently to the margins of politics. The Great Tory Rout of 1997 was not a nadir below which the Tories cannot now fall. Far more probably it was only a great tremor in a continuing electoral collapse that will bury the Conservative Party irrecoverably. Within a generation or less the Conservatives are likely to cease to exist even as a party capable of forming an opposition. That is the real prospect the Tories face today. If the argument of this Conclusion is sound there is no way of avoiding it.

The Great Tory Rout rout of May 1st had many causes. Some of them were avoidable errors, some acts of fortune; some arose from actions or events of the past few years, others were a working out of longer historical trends. It may be worth recalling some of these before turning to what the dissolution of conservatism means for the future of British politics. The dissolution of conservatism was underway palpably in the governments of John Major. He was put in as Tory leader after the coup against Margaret Thatcher in 1990 to do two things: to get rid of the poll tax and sign the Maastricht Treaty. Once this agenda had been accomplished he was rudderless.

Major returned to the only thing he knew. He set Thatcherism on autopilot. He engineered a series of mechanical privatisations, most of them unnecessary and none of them popular, some even lacking in perceptible fiscal benefits to the state. Where privatisation was not feasible he marketised. He injected market mechanisms into public services and intermediary institutions that hitherto had been autonomous and self-regulating. He fell back on the most doctrinaire and unimaginative Thatcherite policies. He did so not from ideological conviction but from the lack of it – and an inaptness for strategic political thinking which he shared with his advisers. Thus it was that an administration reviled by Thatcherites became, in many of its domestic policies, more Thatcherite than Thatcher.

It is commonly argued that the decline of Major's government began with Britain's ejection from ERM in the autumn of 1992. We are told that that fiasco destroyed the faith of voters in Tory economic competence. This conventional narrative fails to capture what it was in Britain's forced departure from ERM that fatally weakened the Major administration of 1992–97. John Major's surprise victory in the general election of 1992 did not reflect voter's confidence in the capacity of his government to manage the economy effectively. It occurred in the middle of a recession. It reflected the fact that more than a decade of Thatcherite rhetoric had succeeded in decoupling voters' view of the performance of the economy from their judgment of the competence of government. As a result many voters no longer held the government accountable for the economy's performance and explained the recession of 1992 as an effect of world market conditions. One of the central goals of early Thatcherite policy – to break the link in the public culture between the business cycle and the electoral cycle – had thereby been achieved.

No doubt the ERM débâcle weakened confidence in the government's economic competence among some voters; but its most fateful effect was to rekindle sectarian conflict in the Conservative Party. The uneasy truce in the cabinet and the Commons between Thatcherites and others was ended. From late 1992 the Thatcherites in Major's cabinet saw themselves as serving an alien government. Their strategic political interest was no longer in a Conservative victory. They became revolutionary defeatists. They saw a Labour victory as a precondition of their regaining control of the Conservative Party. The prospect of electoral catastrophe for the Conservative Party did not enter their calculations.

The governments of John Major never possessed anything resembling a strategy. They were unending exercises in fumbling crisis-management. Major's leadership never shook off the air of farce that it acquired with his ill-advised flirtations with moral fundamentalism in the 'Back to Basics' campaign. His own temperament made recovery more difficult. His stubborn and indecisive leadership turned the odour of sleaze that clung to the government into a stench of decomposition. The electoral coalition assembled by Margaret Thatcher was casually scattered by policies which broke promises on taxes. These were signal defaults of leadership.

Yet it would be a travesty to lay on John Major the principal responsibility for what happened on May 1st 1997. His authority was compromised from the start. The circumstances in which he became leader denied him the legitimacy that had been taken for granted by Conservative leaders in the past. One of the most notable casualties of Thatcher's leadership was the old Tory culture of loyalty. By repudiating the whole of post-war conservatism she divided the Tory tribe. Now it was not a single party culture, but two – made up those who were 'one of us', and the rest. The test which decided who was who was partly loyalty to Thatcher herself. Partly, though, it was a matter of doctrinal commitment. You were 'one of us' if you held to the crankish world view that had been cobbled up by ideologues of the New Right.

In this purblind view of things the post-war consensual Toryism of Butler, Macleod and Macmillan was only an interlude on the way to a socialist state; the responsibilities of the state did not include concern with social cohesion; and Britain's destiny lay across the Atlantic, not with other European countries. By turning a Tory culture of loyalty to the leader into one of doctrinal conformity Thatcher changed the Conservative Party irreversibly. She made it impossible that any future Tory leader should possess the unchallenged legitimacy in the party she had inherited in

1975. John Major was the first Tory leader, but certainly not the last, to have to face the consequences of Thatcher's importation of a sectarian style of politics into the Conservative Party, long familiar on the Labour Left.

In any obituary of conservatism the decay of its party organisation must be mentioned. Party membership has been falling since the 1950s. It halved between 1992 and 1997. As with much else in the party's current condition many of the causes probably goes back to the triumphal 1980s. Perhaps it was then that reliance on large donations from a few wealthy backers came to supplant rather than supplement the contributions of the mass of individual members. For the Tories, during the past five years, electoral collapse and the disintegration of the party machine have gone in tandem. The average age of party members is now in the early sixties. In the local elections of May 1995 the Tories lost over 2,000 councillors. Aside from leaving the Conservatives the third party in British local government, the effect of that cull was to decimate their ranks of Conservative Party activists. In many parts of the country a local party machine barely exists. By contrast, Labour's membership has doubled since Blair became leader in 1994. Now, for the first time, largely as a result of the programme of democratisation driven through by Blair, Brown and Mandelson, Labour's membership exceeds that of the Conservative Party.

It has become conventional wisdom to compare the difficulties facing the Conservative Party in the late 1990s with those confronting Labour in the early 1980s. This is a mistake. The Tories' problems are far worse. Unlike the

Tories, Labour never lost its municipal heartlands or its strength in Scotland and Wales. It is true that Labour's share of the national vote was smaller in 1983 than that of the Tories in 1997; but that was after Labour had split following the Social Democrat's Limehouse Declaration of January 1981. The Conservative electoral collapse of 1997 did not come as a bolt from the blue. The party had not won a by-election for years. It had been almost wiped out in local government and the European parliament. Against this background, it is clear that salvation will not come to the Tories through any swing of the electoral pendulum. Indeed, in present circumstances, the loss of a few more by-elections could well prove fatal.

In the final anaylsis the rout of May 1st was an inescapable nemesis. It was the fate of a party undone by ideological hubris. No ideology can track the paradoxes that animate political life today. Suspicion of ideological thinking used to be one of the virtues of conservative philosophy; but the Conservative Party chose to surrender this suspicion at just the moment when world-historical events rendered all the received political ideologies finally useless. The Tories threw their lot in with an ideology that belonged firmly to the nineteenth century. This New Right ideology was not a species of conservatism. It was the the libertarian doctrine of Herbert Spencer, as revived in more recent times by Hayek, Friedman and others. It was – as Hayek always insisted – an alternative to conservatism. It is often called neo-liberalism, but a more fitting description of New Right ideology is paleo-liberalism. It is classical liberalism reduced to a few simple formulae. In the delirium of the 1980s, in which the

Soviet system was coming apart and Keynesian policies were everywhere in retreat, it seemed to many Conservatives that this curious relic was an idea whose time had come.

Central among the world events that seemed to support this belief was the Soviet collapse. When it occurred it was seen by the New Right as yet another triumph of the free market over central economic planning. In reality the fall of Soviet communism was a geopolitical earthquake whose consequences will be felt for generations. These long-term effects will be as profound and as unsettling for 'Western' societies as they have proved to be for post-communist 'transitional' countries. Already they encompass the unravelling of the settlements and projects that underpinned post-war political life in several Western countries. In Italy the dominant post-war political force, Christian Democracy, has vanished entirely. There are post-communists, post-socialists and even post-fascists; but no post-Christian-Democrats. As a definite regime, European social democracy was an artefact of the Cold War. It has ceased to exist in Sweden and is in retreat everywhere except Norway. In the United States, the Right's hegemony during the Reagan era is a fading historical memory. In France the Right is in deep disarray. In Germany the long tenure in power of a conservative coalition is nearly over. And there cannot be much doubt that the project of a single European currency, unwaveringly supported by the political élites of both France and Germany, is now foundering. It belongs, with the rest of European federalism to the post-war era of a divided Europe that the Soviet collapse brought to a close. For conservatives the implications are ominous. In the past conservatism was animated by enmity to socialism. Today its identity is formed by opposition to European institutions. If, as seems likely, the European project fails, what will conservatism be about? What will the Conservative Party be for?

The Soviet collapse has not inaugurated an era in which the Left is in permanent opposition and the tenets of the paleo-liberal Right are universally accepted. It has triggered a meltdown of post-war regimes and ideas in which the crisis of conservatism is every bit as terminal as that of socialism. The old ideological distinctions between Left and Right have lost most of their usefulness. They are inheritances of the French Revolution. They have no future in the world that has arisen since 1989.

New Right ideas have some particularly disabling limitations. The central assumption was that people value rising incomes and increased consumer choice over all other goods that governments can affect. Strangely, it did not occur to Conservatives who framed policy on this assumption that people – and, more especially, voters – care more about the control of economic risk than they do about rising incomes. Many people are ready to trade off a high income that is rising fast for one that is lower but steadier. Ordinary people have an attachment to economic security that in the narrow terms of New Right theories must seem incongruous.

In part, no doubt, it is the crudity of the New Right's economic model that explains the blindness of Conservatives to the importance of economic insecurity. A better understanding of *homo economicus* – or, for that matter, a passing acquaintance with common experience – would have reminded them that perceptions of risk and uncertainty are central in human conduct, economic and otherwise. But many of the disabilities of New Right thinking are more fundamental than the evident flaws in its economic theories. They arise directly from the origins of classical liberalism in the Enlightenment.

Traditional conservatism, in Burke, Disraeli and Coleridge, was a reaction against the view of human beings taken by the *philosophes* of the Enlightenment. Latter-day conservatism is a caricature of that Enlightenment view. It conceives of human beings in the abstract categories of rational choice. In this empty vision, human beings are merely rational maximisers of their interests. They have histories and communities only by accident. This rationalistic conceit neglects the truth – well understood by traditional conservative thinkers – that it is what is most particular about human beings, not what is universal among them, that gives them their identities. We are who we are, not in virtue of what we have in common, but because of accidents of language and history that make us different from other people.

Like vulgar Marxists, New Right ideologues soon cease to see others as members of a culture they share. They come to see people from the outside. To view one's own culture from this standpoint of detachment might be helpful to an anthropologist. It might enable him to observe the ways of our own society as he would the habits of a remote land. For a Tory philosopher to view his own culture as a foreign country might be considered eccentric. For practising Conservative politicians it has proved ruinous.

The detachment of Conservatives from the common experience of their own society does not come only from their adherence to a closed ideology. It reflects many more practical circumstances. Eighteen years in power encouraged Conservatives to mistake familiarity for stability. At the end of their period in power the Tories were as divorced from the main body of society as the nomenclaturists of communist countries (though considerably less talented and much inferior in political skill and realism). It was only this distance from ordinary people that allowed them to overlook how widely and intensely they were despised.

It was the nomenclatural culture in which the Tories had enclosed themselves that permitted them to see themselves as spokesmen for the prejudices of an inarticulate majority. It did not occur to them that the silent majority for which they pretended to speak might not be a conservative one. They are reminiscent of no one so much as Joseph de Maistre, the great French reactionary thinker, who travelled to Russia in search of a people not yet 'scribbled on' by Enlightenment *philosophes*. He found a population speaking French in the accent of Voltaire.

British Tories have made a similar, if rather less adventurous, journey of discovery. The 1997 general election disclosed a people that cares about public services as much as it does about levels of personal taxation, that is tough on crime but out relaxed on issues of sexuality and family life, that is cautious and genuinely sceptical about European institutions but shares few of the nationalist phobias that fuel Tory Euroscepticism. The general election revealed to the Tories a liberal majority whose existence they had not suspected. The attitudes and beliefs of this unknown people are closer to those of the reviled chattering classes than they are to the poses struck by High Tory intellectuals.

Tory England was once a living, flesh-and-blood reality. It was destroyed by global economic changes and by the social effects of Conservative economic policies. It lingered on in the 1990s as a confection of the 'Little England' media, only to be blown away by the election. Like de Maistre, the Tories have discovered that the country of their imagination does not exist.

The effect on Conservatives of this discovery has not so far been salutary. They have not altered their views to take account of the British liberal majority that declared itself on May 1st. Instead they have drifted into a sort of right-wing multiculturalism. They have set themselves up as spokesmen (they are nearly all men) for a murky rainbow coalition of disaffected minority groups. Hunters and shooters have been anointed as martyrs to a new tyranny of the majority. The contemporary liberal rhetoric of minority rights, which was scorned and ridiculed in the days of Conservative hegemony, has been appropriated as a weapon to be used against legislation seeking to embody the moral common sense of the nation. It cannot be long before John Stuart Mill is canonised as a closet Tory.

These sorry posturings tell us that the instincts of the Tory party are no longer those of a party seeking power. They are better adapted to a permanent existence on the margins of politics. In this, at least, the Tories exhibit an understanding of the present. Their warm embrace of lost causes tells us that they perceive, however dimly, that late modern Britain cannot be the site of a Tory project. Their own policies have collaborated with the most powerful forces of the age to do away with the social order in which Tory statecraft could be effective.

Free markets disrupt traditions and nullify the authority of the past. They dissolve inherited hierarchies and make status in society permanently provisional. They elevate personal choice over all other values. By subjecting people to a continuing imperative of job mobility they make settled communities and enduring relationships harder to sustain. In the real world, if not in the secluded study of the Tory philosopher, free markets work against traditional Tory values. Conservatism has foundered on this contradiction.

The hegemony that the Conservative Party, exercised in British politics for more than a century and a half, depended on its skill in renewing a particular kind of social order. Generations of Tory statecraft bound the Conservative Party by unnumbered threads to institutions and interests central in the life of the nation. Its dominance in national politics reflected its success in building and protecting networks that linked it with centres of power in the country at large. The hegemony of the Conservative Party stood on its successful construction of a Tory Britain. The effect of nearly twenty years of New Right policies, in conjunction with vast changes in the global economy, has been to blow over that construction.[50]

It is odd that there are Conservatives who still deny that free markets can undermine important social institutions. The Conservative Party is notable among the institutions which the free market has undone. The history over the past twenty years of the Conservative Party itself demonstrates the falsity of its ruling ideology.

The paleo-liberal doctrines which Conservatives imbibed in the 1980s told them such conflicts between free markets and social cohesion are illusory or trifling.[51] Provided the British state retired from most of its post-war activities there need be no serious clash between the demands of a deregulated economy and the requirements of social stability. The British electorate has shown that it thinks otherwise, and it is not mistaken.

The historical exemplar on which all paleo-liberal prescriptions are founded shows these conflicts to be all too real. The United States is rightly admired for its technological virtuosity and its economic resourcefulness. It is not commonly revered for its social cohesion. Some of the causes of the exceptionally high levels of breakdown of families and communities in the United States may be local, indigenous and peculiarly American. But some undoubtedly express the social strains of a radically individualist economy. The American example proves that the conflict between free markets and social stability is genuine.

The dogma of minimum government presupposes that free markets and a stable society are never at odds. If, however, they can be in conflict, government must do more than act as umpire of market competition and a guarantor of minimum social standards. It must be active in nurturing social cohesion. It cannot shelter the economy from the gale of world competition. A global free market is an unrealisable utopia; but economic globalization is an unalterable reality.[52] For us globalization is a historical fate. No policy that fails to accept and act on this truth stands any chance of success. Neither social democracy nor protectionism are viable in this new global environment. There is no route back to the world as it was before globalization began to accelerate a generation ago.

It is far from being inevitable that the world's diverse market economies will converge on the business culture of American capitalism. Nor is it desirable. Yet if they are to prosper, economies everywhere will have to adopt more flexible working practices. The cause is not primarily the intensification of market competition by global free trade. It is technological innovation, which has thrown the social division of labour into a flux more unstable than any that has existed since the Industrial Revolution. In these new circumstances the task of government cannot be to protect the economy from change and competition.

In such a context, the responsibility of government is to cultivate institutions that foster social stability. This does not mean returning to the past. Old-fashioned Tories made the mistake of thinking that social stability means the restoration of a traditional social order. Even if that were desirable, which is more than doubtful, it is not possible. The crust of custom is broken. Perhaps that is why some notable Conservatives have concluded that there is no such thing as society. They cannot imagine stable societies which do not resemble those with which they are familiar in the past.

Some are prepared to argue that a loss of social cohesion is an acceptable price for the benefits delivered by free markets. If that is so we are faced with a stark choice. We can have wealth-creating free markets but not in conjunction with social peace. Paleo-liberal Conservatives often claim that social cohesion arises of itself from the prosperity created by free markets. What they mean is that in comparison with wealth-creation social cohesion does not matter. In Britain today, of course, such a position is electorally suicidal.

In the late modern world there can be no coherent conservative political project. The forces of economic and cultural globalization have scattered traditional societies to the winds. When economies and cultures are mutating and interpenetrating as deeply, as swiftly and as incessantly as they are today, the Right cannot be the voice of tradition. In our world there is no such thing. The continuity of tradition has been breached – in part by the market forces which the Right celebrates. In a post-traditional society the Right can neither cleave to the past nor commit itself to the present. It is fated to oscillate between quixotic attempts to restore a traditional social order and ranting evangelism for the free markets that have helped destroy it.

It is beyond the scope of this Conclusion to consider in detail the policies needed to reconcile, as far as that is possible, free markets with social cohesion. Deliberations about policy are – or should be – highly circumstantial. They must fit the conditions of particular people and their cultures, not aim to supply universal panaceas. Still, enough can be said to distinguish the approach to the role of government accepted by Labour from the doctrinaire theory of the minimum state that still mesmerises Conservatives.

For New Labour the scope and functions of government cannot be decided a priori. Like old-fashioned Tories it thinks that the limits of state action should be determined not by an appeal to first principles but by time, place and circumstance. Labour shares with 'One Nation' Tories a concern with vital human needs that today's neo-liberal conservatives neglect. It insists that human beings care about more than consumer choice. They need a measure of security against economic risk and a sense of membership as well. These needs demand common institutions for their satisfaction.

Labour has absorbed the core insights of conservative philosophy; but that does not mean that it has become conservative. The central claim made by its thinkers is that, in our circumstances, conservatism is an impossibility. Among us, individual autonomy is a pervasive and urgent interest; most of us belong not to one but to several, interpenetrating cultural traditions; there is no traditional social order to which we can, or wish to, return. We will not find security in resisting change. Traditional conservatism was concerned with social cohesion; but it was at best indifferent to the values that hold society together in late modern contexts. For us, a concern with social justice, with making the economy more inclusive and the distribution of opportunities and talents fairer, is not an optional extra in policy. It is what social cohesion means.

We cannot hope for a world in which free markets never endanger social cohesion. The goods we value are not in their natures harmonious. They are often rivals. They become compatible only through intelligent and imaginative policies that seek a balance, never final, between human needs that are often contradictory.[53] No country has resolved the dilemma posed by the conflicting needs of deregulated markets and social cohesion. It is unreasonable to demand any final solution of this dilemma. The problem it poses is not fully soluble. But the belief that there can be a better balance between these needs than that which we endured in the era of the New Right is not unreasonable. It is common sense.

In deserting common sense for crankish doctrines conservatism has detached itself from the society for which it once claimed to speak. This does not mean that there can be no circumstances under which the Conservative Party might for a time recover. It means that its prospects now depend entirely on Labour. The Conservative Party could revive if Labour were to make great mistakes in policy. It could enjoy a change in fortune if Labour suffered a run of serious bad luck. In politics, fortune can be nearly all. But not quite everything. Perhaps, after yet another change of leader, the Conservative Party can hope to avoid a precipitate slide into oblivion. But it cannot hope to put Tory Britain back together. That has been broken into pieces − partly by Conservative policies. Tory Britain is gone for good. With it has gone the future of conservatism.

Part IV:
Conclusion
by David Willetts

Emperor Hirohito told the Japanese people in July 1945 that, 'developments have not entirely proceeded as planned'. That is rather how I feel looking back at what I wrote in Part II. But the difficult questions I tried to confront are not dead. Indeed the Conservative Party's electoral defeat makes it even more important that Conservatives refute the extraordinary caricatures of free market conservatism which have done our Party so much damage over the past few years.

One of the key reasons why the Conservative Party lost in 1997 is that many voters took the Conservative belief in the free market to mean that they were willing to destroy institutions and traditions which the electorate hold dear. It has become fashionable for politicians to offer a story of a conversation which brought home to them a crucial political point whilst out canvassing. My example would be knocking on the door of a house in Havant. The lady who answered used to vote Conservative but now she says, 'I call you Conservatives the demolition squad'. This is an absurd position for the Conservative Party to have got itself into.

Labour's first charge was that free market ideology was destroying the 'One Nation'. Their second was that paradoxically it was not even economically efficient. They claim that social cohesion and 'community' is the way to raise our economic performance. One might call this Labour's double whammy. Blair claims that it is Labour which can combine social cohesion and economic efficiency. This is the political battleground which Labour has seized and which the Conservatives must regain.

Underneath the shifting debates on particular issues, one

can identify two central aspirations of the contemporary British citizen. First, we want freedom and opportunity – to feel that we can make life better for ourselves and our families. The most practical expression of this is that we hope to enjoy a rising standard of living. We expect cars to improve, shops to get brighter, magazines to become livelier, hi-fi to continue to get cheaper and our choice of holidays to become wider. We want to feel that as consumers we are sovereign and that if the goods or services we buy are shoddy we can take our custom elsewhere. This is the power of the consumer in a modern free market economy: mobile, free, individualistic. Such a society is based on contract not status. It is strenuous, striving and enterprising.

We want something else too – to know that we have roots and are not just leading a life which is a series of meaningless acts of consumption strung together. We want to be linked to the past through traditions and institutions that are far bigger than any individual. We want to live in a society where people matter to each other, not because we are Mother Theresas, giving up everything to care for other people, but because experiences which are shared are often more real and more satisfying. We do not want to share our property in pursuit of some egalitarian vision but we do want to feel that we are part of one nation where the success and the travails of the royal family, or sportsmen and women, or indeed the stars of the popular soaps, give us something which we share with others and can talk about with them. We want a society where there are thick social ties, not one which has been finely graded into individual grains moving frictionlessly past each other. We want a society of history and traditions, cohesiveness and community.

Each one of us in our own lives is trying to balance these two conflicting pressures. Do you move house to get a better job if it means leaving your friends and disrupting your child's education? Do you drive and shop at the out-of-town superstore or pay a bit more at the local shop? Do you split up from your partner when you are having a bad time or do you think it is a long-term relationship which you ought to stick at through a rough patch?

These are not just personal questions. This tension is at the heart of much political theory. It is the tension between *Gesellschaft* – the anonymous structure of transactions and rules in a modern free market society – and *Gemeinschaft* – the close ties of community where understandings do not have to be explicit because they are so deeply shared. These two principles can both be traced far back in the tradition of conservative thought. The excitement and dynamism of conservatism this century has been generated by a creative tension between these two principles – our belief in individual freedom, private property and the market economy on the one hand, and on the other a commitment to maintaining the institutions which hold our nation together.

It would be a failure of imagination for a political party to tell the British people that they can only have half of what they want – either the fruits of economic success or the rootedness of a long-established society. The extraordinary political success of conservatism this century has come from offering the most coherent and credible account of how to combine these two expectations. It is essential to its political success in the next century.

One way in which conservatives have tied their commitment to property rights and a market economy into a wider ethical scheme has been through an appeal to Christian duty. In a powerful address to the Church of Scotland, Margaret Thatcher tackled head on the charge that her commitment to the free market meant she had no wider sense of social obligation, placing her belief in the free market within a biblical framework. It was how she resolved the question in her own mind – and it was an issue of which she was acutely aware:

> Most Christians would regard it as their personal
> Christian duty to help their fellow men and women.
> They would regard the lives of children as a precious
> trust. These duties come not from any secular legislation
> passed by Parliament, but from being a Christian ... the
> Tenth Commandment – Thou shalt not covet –
> recognises that making money and owning things could
> become selfish activities. But it is not the creation of
> wealth that is wrong, but love of money for its own sake.
> The spiritual dimension comes in deciding what one
> does with the wealth ... any set of social and economic
> arrangements which is not founded on the acceptance of
> individual responsibility will do nothing but harm.[54]

I wish that that was the last word and resolved the issue for us all. But in an increasingly secular society Conservatives cannot simply rely on an appeal to religious belief to persuade people that we know how best to resolve these tensions. Far from successfully defending this territory we have allowed the Labour Party over the past three years to occupy even more of this ground. Commentators actually treat Tony Blair seriously when he talks of a 'One Nation' Labour Party, rights matched with responsibilities and of course 'community'. His success in seizing large chunks of the British political vocabulary has led to his success in seizing large chunks of Parliamentary seats.

Is this just to say that Labour have copied from the Conservatives, stealing our clothes and leaving us politically naked? This is a charge which many Conservatives level at the Labour Party. But it is wrong to say that Labour have been simply copying. For a start it is a serious political mistake – it does not exactly leave much for Conservatives to do unless they migrate to the wilder shores of libertarianism. Fortunately, it is not true either. Blair is indeed after some way of tying individual pursuit of personal interest into a wider vision of community. But his attempt is very different from the authentic conservative approach. A comparison between Britain's main political parties is like comparing coffees or whiskies – they are blends but each is different and distinctive. 'Civic conservatism' is my attempt at setting out that distinctive conservative blend as I understand it. The rest of this conclusion tries to point out the differences between it and Blair's 'New Labour', because these differences are crucial and may help to show how Conservatives can regain the political advantage in years to come. I will begin by looking briefly at Labour's rhetoric and then at some real-live policy issues.

Blair talks a great deal about community, as I myself have

done, heavily influenced by the entirely persuasive communitarian critique of John Rawls' *Theory of Justice*.[55] But the trouble with 'community' is that it is rather soft and formless. A community is an invertebrate form of social life. Conservatives are more interested in communities that have backbones – called institutions. A very similar comparison can be made between Blair's soft soap about 'values' and a more tough-minded belief in 'principles'.

Communities can be rather amorphous, so Labour believe they need to be given shape and structure. This comes from 'partnership', another crucial word in the New Labour vocabulary. And on the other side of the partnership is the state. The state's job becomes to identify communities and then assist them by political action. Often these programmes will be national and end up imposing a uniformed scheme on diverse local communities. There is no clear principle limiting the role of the state in forming 'partnerships' with 'communities'. Moreover Labour's language of 'stake-holding' seems almost intended to blur the traditional legal and political restraints on everyone getting involved in other people's business.

Civic conservatism by contrast is about autonomy for institutions. They may be private and voluntary, though some may be public and tax-financed. Real institutions such as firms or charities, schools or hospitals, have bone and gristle that may be missing from a 'community'. This is why they do not necessarily need or want 'partnerships' with the state or anyone else. They certainly cannot be standardised into one uniform national model.

It is no accident that Labour finds itself drawn down these

paths. They want to pursue an agenda of 'equality' and 'fairness'. The unbearable untidiness of individual independent institutions gets in the way. They want to plan that services are distributed evenly and equally. Inevitably the planning and the distribution of funding has to be done at a much higher level than an individual institution. So they end up with a model in which the planners are supreme and the individual institutions have to be flattened into uniformity and submission.

The trouble is that this goes against the grain of human loyalties and against historical experience. For every one person in my constituency who knows where the local education office or the Health Commission is situated, there are one hundred who know about their local school or GP practice. It was the school and the hospitals which came first, not the education authority and the NHS. To try to run an organisation with the big decisions resting with those superior planning bodies cuts across the principle of power residing with the local institutions which local people recognise and respect.

Communities can also be very intolerant. They may soon start claiming fundamental rights and this is often a way of avoiding negotiation and compromise with others. Communities may have a set of universalist ethical standards and it can be difficult for them to limit their activities to allow space for others. By contrast it is much more difficult for an institution to adopt such a universalist and unqualified language. Institutions find it easier to tolerate each other than communities do.

Before Blair came to power these arguments were

inevitably abstract and hypothetical but now we are beginning to get practical evidence from Labour in office. We can look at the evidence from Labour policy in schools, businesses and jobs.

Let us start with schools. Anyone taking a train across south London, seeing the schools standing high above the surrounding terraced housing, can understand the Victorian vision of the relationship between a school and its neighbourhood – as one commentator pointed out it is like a medieval church in a village. The Royal Commission on the State of Popular Education in 1861 has expressed, as well as anyone, the belief in the power of parental choice and the importance of individual schools shaping their own characters:

> It is a subject of wonder how people so destitute of education as labouring parents commonly are, can be such just judges as they also commonly are of the effective qualifications of a teacher. Good school buildings and the apparatus of education are found for years to be practically useless and deserted when, if a master chanced to be appointed who understands his work, a few weeks suffice to make the fact known, and his school is soon filled, and perhaps found inadequate to the demand of the neighbourhood, and a separate girls' school or infant school is soon found to be necessary.[56]

The conservative vision is to give schools as much autonomy as possible so that they can then shape their own characters. This diversity of schools then gives parents real choice. The government's role is to set basic standards and publish information about schools' performances which helps parents choose what they want for their child. It is not for the government to endorse the path an individual school may take. That is why I deliberately give the example in Chapter 15 of a headmistress who incurred popular opprobrium for refusing to take her pupils to see *Romeo and Juliet* because of its 'blatant heterosexism'. Provided parents were genuinely free to choose I do not believe it is for government to interfere in such a case.

The role of the local education authority is to supply those services which individual schools cannot or do not want to provide for themselves. If the local education authority throws its weight around too much, schools could escape by becoming grant-maintained. This threat of exit may have raised the performance of LEAs because they knew they had to behave sensitively or would otherwise lose control over their schools altogether.

Tony Blair came to office saying this his priority was 'Education. Education. Education'. Labour have moved fast and already published a White Paper on schools. The rhetoric is about raising standards: no-one can be against that. The important question is how this is to be achieved. Time and again the White Paper makes it clear that the Labour government believes the way to raise standards is for local education authorities to reclaim power over schools which they have lost and, even more significantly, for the Department for Education and Employment to have a greater role in controlling schools than ever before in its history. There is in education, as in the rest of public policy, a limited amount of power to go around. Labour's basic approach, hidden behind the soft selling language of 'partnership' to raise 'standards', is for schools and headteachers to be free to do less and for LEAs and the DfEE to gain back the power to do more. They want to give power to the people who plan and take it away from those who do.

So let us come back to the difference between Labour's vision of 'community' and the Conservative civic vision. Instead of being abstract, I can now give a good example of it as a very practical question: is a significant increase in the powers of local education authorities and the DfEE over schools going to make schools stronger or weaker in the local community? If you think the interests of the local community are best expressed through the politicians serving on the local education authorities and nationally at the DfEE, which is the Labour view, then you will say the answer is yes. But if you think that what matters is the strength and authority of an individual school and an individual headteacher, then you will see that Labour's agenda is a threat to this important civic institution.

Labour's approach to industry offers further support for this argument. Let us start with the cliché that comes up in so much portentous social comment. There is a new global economy in which the gales of international competition threaten even the most prominent of our domestic firms. The question then becomes how best we can regain some security in the face of these economic storms. What role might the state have in protecting us from these storms? One response is to be found in the writings of Robert Reich, Clinton's first Labour Secretary, who has had a great influence on Gordon Brown and Tony Blair, as shown in their welfare-to-work programme and their agenda for education and training.[57] His argument is that there is a role for the state in investing in what the economists call 'human capital'. The better educated and the better trained a workforce the greater our ability to command high wages in a competitive international economy. So far so good. But then the difficult questions start. Imagine you have an unhappy group of unemployed and unskilled people and you want to help them into work. One way to do so is for the public sector to train them so that they have the skills to command a decent wage. On this model you take an unemployed unskilled person, the public sector invests in them to make them an unemployed skilled person, and then they get a job as an employed skilled person. The trouble is that there is virtually no evidence from anywhere around the world that public sector training schemes do much good. Education is a crucial responsibility of the state but training involves the state taking a view about the best skills to earn a commercial return and it simply is not very good at this.

The best way to help the unemployed is very different. You start with that same group of unemployed unskilled people and, perhaps through top-up benefits such as Family Credit, you get them into unskilled employment, even they are paid a low wage which the state tops up. Then the employer and the employee between them invest the money so that they can climb up the jobs ladder and end up as employed skilled people. These public sector training schemes are really an accretion of power to the state: there is virtually no economic evidence that they yield much benefit. The only reason why New Democrats in America and New Labour in Britain flirt with such ideas is that they seem to offer an attractive new role for the state even as other roles have shrunk away. The problem, just as with schools, is the absence of any sense of what the state can and cannot do. It has no sense of the independent responsibility of an individual to build up his own skills or the role of the employer in paying for training, and this is the source of the problem.

How does this tie in with the practical questions of civic conservatism? It suggests that even at the sphere of economic policy governments need to have a clear sense of what their role is and a clear sense of the decisions best left to individuals and business. Again there is one question which captures the distinction between a Conservative vision and the Labour one: is an explicit policy of public investment in training an effective way for the state to strengthen the British economy in the face of global competition? I doubt that it is.

The third example is from the area of jobs and it brings us back to the question of what it is that holds us together as a country and what is the legitimate role of government. Tony Blair and Gordon Brown appeal to the moral obligations we all have as members of 'One Nation' to explain the need to impose a minimum wage. As they see it, it is straightforwardly wrong that anyone in our country should command low pay. But maybe this is the only pay, regrettably, that some people can actually earn in the market-place. So the price that will be paid for the minimum wage will be the exclusion of some people from work altogether. The Conservative model by contrast is to use Family Credit to top up the incomes of people in low-paid jobs so that even if they are not earning much from their work, their total income is higher.

This is not just a British policy dilemma. As Peter Lilley has explained, it is a dilemma seen around the world as the divergence between what skilled manpower can earn relative to unskilled increases.[58] One option, as in Britain and America, is to have an open flexible labour market which finds jobs for unskilled workers but perhaps at low pay. We in Britain then try to top those incomes up with Family Credit. The Continental model is to ban low-paid jobs altogether and as a result to have much higher rates of unemployment. Again we can state the crucial question: is tougher regulation of pay and jobs a good way of making us one nation? The paradox may be that only a government which does not try to regulate the labour market, is able to deliver an inclusive society and extend the opportunity to work as widely as possible.

In Part II, I tried to show that the classic conservative intellectual tradition explains how the free market would be integrated into a wider understanding of what ties us together as a country. The real threat to civil society comes not from the market but from the state. That is the fundamental point which we can lose sight of in Britain because of our optimistic belief in benign, rational, all-knowing government.

This may help generate a political agenda for Conservatives now. The Conservative Party has to reconnect with significant groups of voters who have become alienated from them over the past few years. Civic conservatism may be able to help us do that too. It speaks to teachers, businessmen and the unemployed, and explains why Labour, even New Labour, is a threat whereas Conservatives are on their side. And there are many other groups who will similarly find themselves suffering the depredations of New Labour – people living in the country, pensioners, GP fundholders and their patients. There is a certain prissy bossiness to Blair's Labour Party which will gradually alienate more and more groups. Civic conservatism helps provide the intellectual framework within which Conservatives can make common cause with them.

Perhaps above all, civic conservatism brings us back to that fundamental issue in British politics which has still not gone away. It reminds us that what is distinctive about civic institutions, as opposed to 'communities' in 'partnerships' with government, is that conservatism is about keeping government out of the way.

Acknowledgements

Apart from editorial changes, the 1994 edition of *The Undoing of Conservatism* is republished here unaltered. I am grateful to Roderick Nye for suggesting to me that it might be worth republishing with a new Conclusion. I am also grateful to Andrew Franklin and Nicky White of Profile Books for their help with this new edition.

John Gray
Oxford, 1997

I should begin by thanking the Oxford don under whom I studied political philosophy twenty years ago – John Gray. His views have changed since then and our intellectual paths have diverged, but that original intellectual debt remains.

Daniel Finkelstein, Director of the Conservative Research Department and Roderick Nye, Director of the Social Market Foundation, have both been enormously generous in helping with this project at every stage. They are the shrewdest, sharpest and wisest critics any author could hope for.

I have enjoyed many discussions over the years with Professor Lawrence Mead of New York University and have learned much from him about social policies which work (and those which do not). He is a persuasive advocate of civic culture.

Finally I should like to thank my assistant, Helga Wright, who worked on this project as always with great good humour and dedication.

David Willetts
Havant, 1997

Notes

Part 1: The Undoing of Conservatism

1   F. A. Hayek. *The Constitution of Liberty*, Chicago University Press, Chicago, 1960, p. 41.

2   I have discussed some aspects of commercial expression in my monograph, *Advertising Bans: Administrative Decisions or Matters of Principle?*, Social Affairs Unit, London, 1991.

3   For a good statement of the contemporary New Left position, see Hilary Wainright, *Arguments for a New Left: Answering the Free Market Right*, Blackwell, Oxford and Cambridge, Mass., 1994.

4   I refer, of course, to Michael Oakeshott, and in particular to his essay, 'On being conservative', in *Rationalism in Politics and other Essays*, Liberty Press, Indianapolis, 1991.

5   Edward Luttwak. 'Why Fascism is the Wave of the Future', in *London Review of Books*, 7 April, 1994, pp. 3, 6

6   Adam Smith. *Lectures on Jurisprudence*, Liberty Classics, Indianapolis, 1982, pp. 539-540.

7   Ibid. p. 541.

8   In the subtlest versions of this approach, of which that of James Buchanan is pre-eminent, the drastic simplification involved in the adoption of the homo economicus model of political behaviour is candidly acknowledged. The epistemology underlying this view is clearly instrumentalist or pragmatist. On Buchanan's work, see my 'Buchanan on liberty' in *Post-liberalism: Studies in political thought*, Routledge, London and New York, 1991.

9   These errors have been particularly debilitating to thought and policy in regard to the post-communist societies. On this, see my *Post-Communist Societies in Transition: A Social Market Perspective*, Social Market Foundation, London, 1994.

10 See Sir James Goldsmith, *The Times*, March 5, 1994, for a masterly demolition of the usual arguments for global free trade and a timely warning of its dangers.

11 Herman E. Daly, 'From Adjustment to Sustainable Development: The Obstacle of Free Trade' in *The Case Against Free Trade*, Earth Island Press, San Francisco, 1993, pp. 126-7.

12 On Oakeshott and Santayana, see my book, *Post-liberalism: Studies in political thought*, Routledge, London and New York, 1991, Chapters 2 and 6.

13 That the disposition to constitute for themselves particular local identities is universal among human beings was maintained by J. G. Herder and other thinkers of what Isaiah Berlin terms the Counter-Enlightenment. For an exposition and assessment of such views

in the context of an exploration of Berlin's contemporary attempt to reconcile them with liberalism, see my book *Berlin*, HarperCollins (Fontana Modern Master), London, 1995.

14 M. Oakeshott, *Rationalism in Politics and other Essays*, Liberty Press, Indianapolis, 1991, p.410.

15 On this remarkable case, see my *Post-liberalism*, Routledge, London and New York, 1991.

16 Edward Goldsmith, *The Way: An ecological world-view*, Rider, London, 1992, Chapter 8.

17 George Santayana, *Dominations and Powers: Reflections on Liberty, Society and Government*, Charles Scribner and Sons, New York, 1951, p. 340.

18 On Mill's idea of the stationary state, see my book, *Beyond the New Right: Markets, government and the common environment*, Routledge, London and New York, 1994, Chapter 4.

19 I owe my understanding of the embeddedness of economic institutions in cultural traditions to conversations with Edward Goldsmith.

20 See my *Beyond the New Right*, Routledge, London and New York, 1994, Chapter 3, 'The Moral Foundations of Market Institutions'.

21 I refer to the liberal political philosophy of Joseph Raz, which I have discussed in my *Beyond the New Right*, ibid.

22 I have discussed the untransparency of value, and its implications for liberal theory, in my book, *Post-liberalism*, Routledge, London and New York, 1991, Chapter 20, 'What is dead and what is living in liberalism'.

23 For a statement of this criticism of Raz, see B. Parekh, 'What's wrong with liberalism', *Times Literary Supplement*, February 25, 1994.

24 For a statement of this communitarian view, see Michael Sandel, *Liberalism and the Limits of Justice,* Cambridge University Press, Cambridge, 1982.

25 The best contemporary exposition of this reactionary view is probably Roger Scruton's *The Meaning of Conservatism,* Penguin, London, 1980.

26 I have discussed the idea of a negative capital tax in my *Beyond the New Right*, Routledge, London and New York, 1994, p. 153 ; where I have also criticised neo-liberal proposals for a negative income tax in Chapters 1 and 3.

27 David Ricardo. *Principles of Political Economy and Taxation*, J.M.Dent and Co., London, 1911, pp. 266-67. Ricardo's conclusions about the deleterious impact of machinery on the interests of labourers have been supported by Paul Samuelson in his 'Mathematical Vindication of Ricardo on Machinery' in *Journal of Political Economy*, 96, 1988, pp. 274-82,

and 'Ricardo was Right!' in *Scandinavian Journal of Economics*, 91, 1989, pp. 47-62. An excellent critique of the conventional arguments for free trade is to be found in the papers collected in *The Case Against Free Trade: GATT, NAFTA, and the Globalization of Corporate Power*, San Francisco: Earth Island Press, 1993. I am indebted to Edward Goldsmith for drawing this invaluable book to my attention.

28 Sir James Goldsmith, *The Times*, March 5, 1994.

29 I attempt such a *tour d'horizon* in Chapter 4 of my *Beyond the New Right*, Routledge, London and New York, 1994, Chapter 4. I hold still to most of the views on policy defended there, without wishing to defend them mainly in conservative terms.

30 See my *Beyond the New Right*, Routledge, London and New York, 1994, Chapter 3.

31 I have developed a case for voucher schemes for schools, drawing not on neo-liberal thought but on the work of Ivan Illich, in my *Beyond the New Right*, Routledge, London and New York, 1994, Chapter 4.

Part II: Civic Conservatism

32 Thomas Carlyle. 'Gospel of Mammonism', *Selected Writings*, Penguin, London, 1986, pp. 277–78.

33 Joseph Schumpeter. *Capitalism, Socialism and Democracy*, Unwin, 1943, p. 67.

34 Alan Macfarlane. *The Origins of English Individualism*, Basil Blackwell, Oxford, 1978. The picture in Scotland was different – but this is relevant to other political debates.

35 Alice Coleman. *Utopia on Trial: Vision and Reality in Planned Housing*, Hilary Shipman, 1985.

36 quote from Gertrude Himmelfarb. *Poverty and Compassion: The Moral Imagination of the Late Victorians*, Knopf, New York, 1991, p. 272.

37 Ferdinand Mount. *The British Constitution Now: Recovery or Decline?*, Heinemann, London, 1992.

38 quote from Gertrude Himmelfarb. *Poverty and Compassion: The Moral Imagination of the Late Victorians*, Knopf, New York, 1991, p. 186.

39 One Nation Group, *Change is Our Ally*, Conservative Political Centre, 1954, p. 7.

40 Digby Anderson (ed.). *The Loss of Virtue: Moral Confusion and Social Disorder in Britain and America*, The Social Affairs Unit, 1992.

41 William Julius Wilson. *The Truly Disadvantaged: The Inner City, the Underclass and Public Policy*, University of Chicago Press, Chicago IL, 1987.

42 Charles Murray. *Losing Ground: American Social Policy 1950–1980*, Basic Books, New York, 1984.

43 Richard Freeman. 'Who Escapes? The Relation of Church-going and Other Background Factors to the Socio-economic Performance of Black Male Youths from Inner-city Tracts', in Richard Freeman and Harry Holzer (eds.). *The Black Youth Employment Crisis*, University of Chicago Press, Chicago IL, 1986.

44 Seymour Fleigel. *Miracle in East Harlem: The Fight for Choice in Public Education*, Manhattan Institute, New York, 1993.

45 *Overview of the Seattle-Denver Income Maintenance Experiment, Final Report*, US Dept. of Health and Human Services, 1983.

46 Douglas Hurd. 'Foreword', *Reports to Parliament on European Developments*, Foreign & Commonwealth Office, April 1995.

47 House of Commons Public Accounts Committee, *The Proper Conduct of Public Business*, 8th report, House of Commons Paper No. 154, 1993–94 Session.

48 Stephan Collini. *The Idea of 'Character' in Victorian Political Thought*, Transactions of the Royal Historical Society, 1985, p. 30.

49 David Willetts. *Modern Conservatism*, Penguin, London, 1992.

Part III: Conclusion by John Gray

50 I analysed the causes of the disappearance of Tory England in 'The Strange Death of Tory England', in my book *Endgames: Questions in Late Modern Political Thought*, Polity Press, Cambridge, 1997, Chapter 1. I have examined the contradictions of New Right thought and policy in earlier writings, particularly *Beyond the New Right: Markets, government and the common environment*, Routledge, London and New York, 1994 and *Enlightenment's Wake: Politics and Culture at the Close of the Modern Age*, Routledge, London and New York, 1995.

51 The best statement of this view is articulated by David Willetts in Part II of this book.

52 I discuss the relationship of the historical process of globalization with the utopian political project of a global free market in my forthcoming book, *False Dawn: The utopia of the global free market*, Granta, London, January 1998.

53 The thesis that human values are not harmonious is the central idea of Sir Isaiah Berlin's liberal philosophy. I discuss it in my book, *Berlin*, HarperCollins, London, 1995.

Part IV: Conclusion by David Willetts

54 Margaret Thatcher. Speech made at the General Assembly of the Church of Scotland, May 21st 1988.

55 David Willetts. *Modern Conservatism*, Penguin, London, 1992.

56 Royal Commission on the State of Popular Education, 1861, quoted in E. G. West, *Education and the State: A Study in Political Economy*, Liberty Press, 1994.

57 Robert Reich. *The Work of Nations*, Vintage Books, New York, 1992.

58 Peter Lilley, Lecture to Northern Ireland Conservative Political Centre, November 4, 1995.